MW01053704

"At the heart of this story is Jean Ballon, a woman of extraordinary contradictions—willing to astound and confound with her unbridled independence and salty language, while beneath the surface lie her passionate humanity and deep reverence. I had the great joy of personally witnessing the fullness of her humor, her talents, and her commitment to Judaism; and the honor of calling her my friend. It is little surprise that her departure from life would be the source of this deep and revealing tale of conflict, compassion, forgiveness, and love. Yesh Ballon honors the memory of his mother with this earnest exposition of his family and of his personal spiritual journey."

—DAVID SAPERSTEIN, Director emeritus, Religious Action Center of Reform Judaism, and former US Ambassador-at-Large for International Religious Freedom

"In *Unthinkable Dreams*, Yeshaya Ballon offers a touching, soul-searched memoir that is remarkable for the author's honesty, deep self-analysis, and pinpoint clarity of expression. For anyone who has endured the loss of a loved one or will at some time in the future, Ballon's book will be an instructive and inspiring resource."

—STEPHEN LEWIS FUCHS, former President, World Union for Progressive Judaism, and Rabbi, Bat Yam Temple of the Islands, Sanibel, Florida

"In reading *Unthinkable Dreams*, I fell in love with this family! I observed their devotion to their ailing mother, their grief after her death—intensified by the 9/11 attacks—and their subsequent sibling squabbles. Yesh Ballon delivers a touching and unvarnished story of a family physically and emotionally divided. It was inspiring to witness the journey of faith and love that ultimately reunited them."

—MAGGIE CALLANAN, coauthor of *Final Gifts: Understanding the Special Awareness, Needs, and Communications of the Dying*

"In *Unthinkable Dreams*, Yesh Ballon gives us a personal and thought-provoking eulogy to his mother Jean. In the unfolding of his reflection, we come to learn the arc of his journey, from separation to connection through the window of compassion. We encounter a journey from loss to adjustment and learn lessons about the power of family as well as the art of flexibility and personal growth."

—RICHARD F. ADDRESS, Director, Jewish Sacred Aging

"Yesh Ballon tells a passionate tale of his mother's life and death. It is a personally unique and universally human story of a family wrestling with the complexity of love and loss. Interweaving personal narrative, ritual practices of Jewish tradition, and the reality of life immediately after the 9/11 tragedy, this book is profoundly relevant for all of us dealing with death and grief today."

—SIMCHA RAPHAEL, author of *Jewish Views of the Afterlife*

"In the Torah, our holy Scriptures, our ancestors gave us stories of messy family entanglements because the work we do to forgive, make peace, and receive our legacies forms the foundation for the spiritual work of liberation. *Unthinkable Dreams* sends us to that work. It details a wise and generous process of coming into the fullness of love and wisdom through introspection, reconciliation, and the lifting up of truth. Ballon's story sparkles with clarity, humor, and insight. It sends each of us to the joyful work of receiving our complicated and precious legacies in the spirit of adventure."

—SHEFA GOLD, author of *Are We There Yet? Travel as a Spiritual Practice*

"In *Unthinkable Dreams*, Yesh Ballon tells the story of the death of his remarkably spirited mother, Jean, in the context of both the national tragedy of the 9/11 attacks and of his own spiritual journey as he searches for a Judaism that speaks to the heart as well as to the head. A moving and original exploration of the mourning process, inter-familial relations, and Jewish ritual practice."

—STEVEN SHANKMAN, Professor of English and UNESCO Chair in Transcultural Studies, Interreligious Dialogue, and Peace, University of Oregon

"Storytelling, especially of the deeply authentic, personal-accounting kind, is one of the most powerful ways to illuminate seemingly obvious but not yet understood truths. In *Unthinkable Dreams*, Yesh Ballon offers up his own personal family story to illuminate how healing can happen—when we can move from separation to connection—when we embrace compassion."

—YOSAIF AUGUST, author of *Coaching for Caregivers: How to Reach Out Before You Burn Out* and co-founder of Menschwork

"Yesh Ballon's book about his beloved mother touches the heart. He teaches us to dig deep into the stories, lessons, and connections we have with our loved ones. As we peel back layer after layer, we find more lessons buried in everyday encounters recalled. The struggles honestly described in *Unthinkable Dreams* beautifully exemplify the growth that comes from reflection, confrontation with parts of ourselves we want to reject, and empathy and acceptance. This is a book of healing. It models compassion, forgiveness, and love. It is a treasure."

—NATHANIEL EZRAY, Senior Rabbi, Congregation Beth Jacob,
Redwood City, California

"*Unthinkable Dreams* is the memoir of how one family loved and lost its mother. It tells of how they tended to her in her last days, how they bickered and squabbled with each other under the stress, and how they came to reconcile with each other and with themselves after her death. It is very well written. On almost every page there is a crisp metaphor or a sharply worded truth that makes us sit up and notice. It leaves us with an honest report of how devastating grief can be, and how lonely and isolating it is for a person to walk the road that leads from love to loss."

—JACK RIEMER, author of *Finding God in Unexpected Places* and
The Day I Met Father Isaac in the Parking Lot

"Yesh Ballon has written a candid and fascinating story of how his Jewish family dealt with the death of their mother just two days before the terrorist attacks of 9/11. Along the way, he offers many insights into how families handle the death of a parent. As a Catholic, I recognize, as Yesh does, the value of religious rituals to express grief at a loved one's death and, in some ways, to keep it within bounds. I wholeheartedly agree that our respective religions urge us to forgive and reconcile with our enemies and that compassion toward others—and in some ways, toward ourselves—opens the way to create or repair connections between persons. I think that many Jewish families that have dealt with death will recognize themselves in the particular dynamic of *Unthinkable Dreams*, but that non-Jews too will relate to its deeper themes of grief, family tensions, the urge to reconcile, and the power of religious ritual. I enjoyed reading *Unthinkable Dreams* and I trust others will as well."

—MARK EDWARD BRENNAN, Bishop of Wheeling-Charleston

Unthinkable Dreams

The Year That Mom Died and the Towers Fell

Unthinkable Dreams

The Year That Mom Died and the Towers Fell

YESHAYA DOUGLAS BALLON

Foreword by Malka Drucker and Nadya Gross

RESOURCE *Publications* · Eugene, Oregon

UNTHINKABLE DREAMS
The Year That Mom Died and the Towers Fell

Resource Publications
An Imprint of Wipf and Stock Publishers
199 W. 8th Ave., Suite 3
Eugene, OR 97401

www.wipfandstock.com

PAPERBACK ISBN: 978-1-6667-1411-1
HARDCOVER ISBN: 978-1-6667-1412-8
EBOOK ISBN: 978-1-6667-1413-5

08/19/21

I dedicate this book to my mother, Jean Hymson Ballon—a role model for living one's own life, and for being perpetually fascinated by anything and everything. I am grateful for her giving us an eleventh-hour peek into her soul. Recently, when asked what my motto is, I unhesitatingly replied, "Have fun!" Where else would I have developed such a profound philosophy but from my fun-loving mom? Her zest for creating beauty, for bringing rich flavor to daily living, and for exploration and creativity are gifts that I aspire to pass on to her descendants by living her values and telling her story.

In the foreword to *From Generation to Generation*, a cookbook she edited in 1974, my mother stated what I would deem to be a pithy summation of her philosophy, not only of cooking, but of life: "As long as you must cook, you might as well make it an adventure." She dedicated her cookbook to her children, and to their children. In her name, I lovingly extend that dedication to the generations that follow.

Jean Hymson Ballon, 1979

You don't know what's in a peanut shell 'til you shell it.

—JEAN BALLON

Contents

PART 3: MISHPACHA | CONNECTION

Foreword

In this timely book, Yesh Ballon illustrates the need for compassion in the most difficult moments of life. In facing the death of his mother, which occurred two days before 9/11, he shares with us the loneliness of one man's grief, and how personal anguish is often drowned out by the collective cry.

We understand his alienation because of what we experienced in 2020. This past year taught us the importance of having community to share in our joy as well as to provide consolation in our sorrow. Whether we've suffered our own losses or borne witness to the deaths of more than half a million fellow citizens during this year of COVID, all of us are grieving. Some of us have stood at graveside with just a few family members and have missed the comforting presence of extended family, friends, and community. Others, because of travel and/or public health restrictions, have not been able to be in attendance at all.

Yesh and his family experienced similar isolation two decades before the coronavirus pandemic. His story presages the Zoom rituals many of us have participated in recently, meager substitutes for physical presence.

Although Jean Hymson Ballon's family did have the privilege of being with her as she approached death, they bumped up against the challenges that many of us face within family at times of crisis. The drama intensified after the terrorist attacks, when the Ballons found themselves unable to carry out their agreed-upon funeral plans. Latent sibling rivalries surfaced, intensifying the strife.

Jewish tradition guides us to say: "May Jean's memory be a blessing." In the twenty years since his mother's death, Yesh has found new perspectives that he couldn't have accessed in the immediacy of his loss and during those disturbing days for the country. Lingering resentments from that period dissipated as Yesh sought to glean lessons from the events that led to and followed the death of his mother. This is part of eldering—using the vision and gifts garnered over a lifetime to seek continued growth, understanding, and wholeness. Eldering provides the compassion that moved Yesh from separation to connection, that enabled him to posthumously reconcile with his brother, and that allowed him to fully receive and pass forward the blessings of Jean's memory.

When we suffer a loss, we awaken to the suffering of others who have walked this path before us. Our hearts open and reconnect us. *Unthinkable Dreams* is a guide for all of us, whether we have recently borne the passing of loved ones without the support of community, or whether we have endured a sense of grief and isolation in more normal times. This book reassures us that despite the fact that there is no mitigating the staggering losses of a pandemic, there is a wisdom learned over the years that offers its own consolation. May Yesh Ballon's story bolster within each of us the capacity for compassion, the courage to face old wounds, and the patience and determination needed to heal our sorrows.

Rabbi Malka Drucker and Rabbi Nadya Gross
Authors of *Embracing Wisdom: Soaring in the Second Half of Life*
Passover 2021

Preface

My mother, Jean Hymson Ballon, died on September 9, 2001—two days before the terrorist attacks. Even in death, she found a way to make things a little more interesting than they had to be. This is the chronicle of the discoveries, drama, and occasional delights that my family and I experienced in the days and months before and after Mom's death. All the emotional upheaval that we went through as her health was failing throughout the preceding summer intensified during the traumatic week that followed her death. For me, it took the rest of that year to heal from some of the wounds. Nearly twenty years later, I'm still healing.

Ours is a story of adult siblings dealing with the death of our mother in the face of a national crisis. It describes the hardship of not being able to physically be with one another, to lovingly and respectfully bury our dead, to celebrate her life, or to mourn our loss.

Many people today are facing challenges similar to those we faced decades ago. I am writing this book during a period of upheaval in our nation—unprecedented, at least in my lifetime. The world has been devastated by the COVID-19 pandemic. Many victims of the disease face treatment and even death segregated from their loved ones. Measures to suppress the spread of coronavirus have forced families to hold virtual funerals, much as my family did in 2001 albeit with far less sophisticated technology than is available today. On top of that, in response to documented racial injustice, our nation is experiencing civil unrest at a level unseen in decades. Many African Americans justifiably feel marginalized, violated, and unheard. They have been joined by others in demonstrations crying out for justice.

It is possible that the pain of separation and alienation has never been felt more keenly by more people than it is today. Yet it is my sense that in large part, it is the *awareness* of separation that is heightened. I suspect that feelings of despair lie dormant at all times, undetected in the general population, and that the global pandemic and blatant racism have merely unmasked and unleashed these dormant feelings. It is in the midst of today's environment of uncertainty, anxiety, and fear that I reflect, with nearly two decades of perspective, on my family's experience during another calamitous time in the history of our nation. These periods of upheaval remind us that we all want our voices to be heard; we all thrive on bestowing and receiving compassion; we all crave a sense of belonging. These are universal human needs.

It's hard to lose a parent. It's even more difficult to lose a parent when the world is in chaos. Where does one turn for support if not to those who are closest? Sadly, however, it is often the family members with whom one is closest who become the most difficult during challenging times.

In spring 2001, when it appeared that our mother was in decline, there was no way I could know what our family would be facing for the remainder of the year. I could not anticipate all that was required of adult children supporting a dying mother, or the challenges that would arise among siblings all heading to the same destination via vastly different routes. I had little insight into my growing separation anxiety or the increased yearning for personal and community connection that it would generate. I lacked perspective on my lifelong wrestling with the shadows of my mother's persona, or on the hidden light within her that would be emerging. I also was the son of a rabbi who had died nearly three decades before. Although I knew I was still wrestling with that relationship, I was unaware of how it was inextricably interwoven with issues I faced with my mother.

An important part of this journey was discovering how to listen to our mother speak when objectively, a lot of what she was saying made little sense to us. Over the course of the summer of 2001, when I visited Mom, she would carry on with ample conversation. Often, it seemed as if she were hallucinating or free associating. We learned that we shouldn't dismiss everything she said out of hand. Much of her words could be allegorical, subject to interpretation as one might interpret symbols in a dream by looking for images that convey meaning. Deep listening, especially under these circumstances, was essential. It was a time in which my relationship with Mom seemed to blossom, even as her body and mind withered.

In his landmark book *From Age-ing to Sage-ing*, written in his sixtieth year, Rabbi Zalman Schachter-Shalomi described his thoughts about approaching the "third act" of life, sometimes referred to as "eldering." Among his wise teachings were to make peace with the past by recontextualizing events that at the time may have seemed hurtful, but later could be seen to have provided important benefits or lessons. Learning from Reb Zalman, I have turned over and over the story of my dying mom and my grieving family to mine it for its meaning and messages, looking for some fundamental truths, some bits of wisdom. Nearly twenty years after these events took place, I find that by telling and retelling this story, I continue to discover aspects of our behavior that were not evident to me at the time. Some of these observations cause me to cringe, even as they inspire me to learn, grow, and, God-willing, do better should I find myself in a similar situation.

Reb Zalman encouraged those in the autumn of their years not only to harvest meaning from the past, but to plant seeds, to leave a legacy for the future. It is my fervent hope that the story of Jean Ballon contributes to her legacy as well as to my own.

As I contemplate those months that surrounded Mom's passing, I am struck by three overarching themes. I explore these themes in the three sections of this book: *Separation, Compassion,* and *Connection.* Within that structure are eighteen chapters, each beginning with one of my chronologically arranged journal entries. We start with September 11 and the days that followed the attack, and end on the last week of December 2001. These were two dark periods of that year, but they were dark for very different reasons. September was a somber time in American history; whereas darkness in December was due to the winter solstice. Dark as those December days were, they provided a reprise of my mother's spiritual light, and a measure of healing for our family.

Following each journal entry are reflections, observations, and flashbacks primarily from the months preceding Mom's death, as well as glimpses of our family from earlier times. The occasional poems are mine, except as noted. In each section of the book, I look through a different lens. I often revisit certain days of Mom's final summer, but I focus on different details, thereby gleaning additional insights. It's a journey from separation to connection by way of compassion, and the route is neither straight nor continuous.

Family Tree

The partial Hymson family tree below, showing Mom's closest relatives, will be useful to the reader in establishing the basic relationships of those people introduced throughout the narrative.

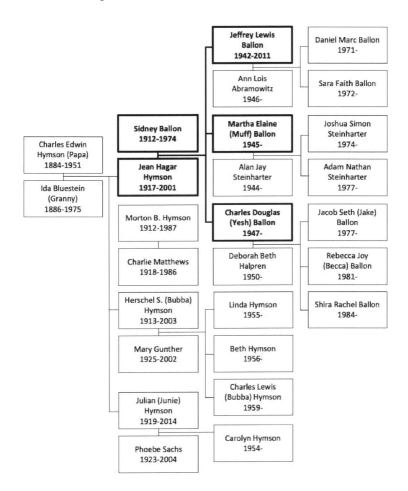

Acknowledgments

There is no story to tell without my sister, Martha (Muff) Ballon Steinharter, and her tireless efforts to support our mother during the challenging period documented herein. Now that so many years have passed, and our brother, Jeffrey, is also gone from our midst, Muff and I have only one another to turn to for corroboration of these events and even more distant family memories. I was grateful to be at her side through the tears and the laughter.

In his final days, Jeff went on a relentless crusade delivering blessings and a message about the power of love to all he met. I am ever grateful for his teaching.

I thank Debbie, my wife of more than fifty years, for recommending that Muff and I read the book *Final Gifts: Understanding the Special Awareness, Needs, and Communications of the Dying* by Maggie Callanan and Patricia Kelley. It gave us insight into Mom's otherwise enigmatic ramblings, and opened a world of understanding and comfort that would not otherwise have been realized. Debbie's wise and gentle presence was especially needed and appreciated throughout the events described in this book.

Many declare that Debbie perennially deserves a medal for putting up with me. As I worked on the book, she was subjected to my endless chatter about the roadblocks and the great epiphanies that I stumbled upon day and night. Moreover, she kindly gave the book a careful reading, and *bravely* offered many useful editorial suggestions. (I never err listening to my beloved wife!) Most of all, she has been a fountain of nurturing and love during her lifetime devotion to our family. She is a blessing.

Thanks go to Jacob Ballon, my son, for showing up in a big way. He was a great source of support and comfort to his grandmother in her final months and to those of us at her bedside. I thank his wife, Alana Kadden Ballon, for insightful suggestions on how to improve this book. I am indebted to Becca & Josh Shapiro, and to Shira Ballon & Marty Scigouski—my daughters and their husbands—for their continuous love and support. I am grateful for the entire extended family who were a part of Mom/Granny/Aunt Jean's life.

It's difficult to piece together memories that span a lifetime. I thank those friends and family who shared some of their recollections of Mom to fill out the portrait I have tried to paint of her. These include Beth Ayer, Ann Lois Ballon, Sara Ballon, Carolyn Gilbert, Nancy Gottlieb, Joe Loewy, Judi Narrowe, Judith Plaskow, Marc Seifer, Becca Shapiro, Murray Simon, Adam Steinharter, and Alan Steinharter.

During the two decades between the unfolding of this story and the writing of the book, my Jewish education and spiritual life has undergone significant growth. In 2007, I discovered ALEPH: Alliance for Jewish Renewal. I will be ever appreciative of and grateful to my many instructors and classmates in The Sage-ing® Legacy Program (now part of Yerusha), the Davennen' Leadership Training Institute (DLTI), Kol Zimra—Chant Leaders Professional Development, and Hashpa'ah—Training Program for Jewish Spiritual Directors. Thank you also to my friends and colleagues at The Yedidya Center for Jewish Spiritual Direction, and to the compassionate team at the Spiritual Care Service at Stanford Health Care.

I received sage advice from a family friend and professional story consultant, Sam Simkin. In response to his gentle guidance, I've tried to do more than merely narrate the events surrounding Jean Ballon's passing, but also probe for its meaning and spiritual significance.

I owe a huge debt of gratitude to my long-time spiritual mentor and friend Rabbi Howard Avruhm Addison who gave me tools to do that spiritual probing. His astute guidance had a direct impact on shaping both form and substance of the book in more than one of its iterations. In my work with Avruhm over the years, I have learned an approach to harvesting rich meaning from my dreams, and I've been able to apply this technique to probing for deeper understanding of images and events within this narrative.

Once again, I have had the extreme pleasure of working with Dr. Emily Moberg Robinson of Woodshed Editors. Emily did far more than move the commas around my manuscript—and she did plenty of that. She thoughtfully and diligently probed every word, clause, and paragraph for its meaning and message, making subtle suggestions to polish my prose. Emily is a true joy to work with, a great partner in the creative process.

I am blessed to have a cadre of people in my life who directly, indirectly, consciously, or unconsciously showed up in some way that helped me navigate the challenging times surrounding Mom's death, supported the development of the book itself, and/or were spiritual companions along the way: Richard & Andrea Altman, Adrienne Ammen, Robert Badame, Michael Battat, Rabbi Aliza Berk, Benjie Bluestein, Constance Burton, Magdalena Cabrera, John Carlsen, Rabbi Jen Clayman & Rabbi John Fishman, Carla Davis, Steve & Jackie Dines, Adam Donovan, Rabbi Nat Ezray, Aviva

Feintech, Dr. Bruce Feldstein, Bill Futornik, Angela Gold, Rabbi Shefa Gold, Rabbi Ilana Goldhaber-Gordon, Jon & Susan Golovin, Chris Green, Linda Leah Greene, David Greenspan, David Groode, Rabbis Nadya & Victor Gross, Fred & Cherie Half, Calyah Chanah Isaacs, Rabbi Shaya Isenberg & Bahira Sugarman, Lynne Iser, Rabbi Burt Jacobson, Alison Jordan, Kenny Joseph, Rabbi Bruce Kadden, Ken Kaye, Greg Kimura, David Daniel Klipper, Wendie Bernstein Lash, Dan Leemon, Maxine Litwak, Rabbi Sanford Marcus, Rabbi Rachel Marder, Max Mazenko, Rabbi Jim & Julia Mirel, Ken Newman, Michael & Karen Nierenberg, Ben Ovshinsky, Michael Park, Rabbi Charna Rosenholtz, Nate Ross, Rabbi Saul Rubin, Hannah Salanter, Steve & Cheryl Shapiro, Rabbi Paul Shleffar, Lee Shulman, David & Patti Smilovitz, Rabbi Ruth Sohn, Doug & Susan Solomon, Rabbi Jacob Staub, Rabbi Adam Stein, Karen & Elliot Stein, Ellen Stromberg, Rabbi David Teitelbaum, Elia & Halimah Van Tuyl, Penelope Van Tuyl, Adrienne, David & Elana Weil, Gary Weiner, Ira Wiesner, and Rabbi Shawn Zevit.

This book has been enriched by all whom I have mentioned. Its virtues are due in large measure to their wisdom and kindness; its shortcomings—it hardly needs to be said—are all mine. I hope I will be forgiven if I have inadvertently omitted a contributor.

Part 1
Havdalah

הבדלה

Separation

Death—it won't come soon enough to do me any good.

—Jean Ballon

SEPARATION

In Hebrew, the word for separation is *havdalah*. It is also the name of the ceremony at the end of the Sabbath that marks its separation from the ordinary days of the week. It is said that every death—no matter how long it has been anticipated—is a *sudden* death. The moment of death marks a *havdalah*—a separation from life.

The stories herein relate the events that preceded and followed that unique moment for my mother. *Havdalah* becomes particularly meaningful in our story, because after the physical and emotional separations that were caused by Mom's death and the subsequent terrorist attacks, months later our family finally had the opportunity to reconnect at a *havdalah* ceremony held in her memory.

Separation isn't necessarily a bad thing. From time to time, we all need opportunities to be alone for relaxation or for productivity. In dealing with my mother's deteriorating condition and ultimate death, I occasionally found the respite I needed in different forms of meditation and in grabbing the time and space to journal. It was a form of separation that provided great comfort. There were times when I was disconnected from my own feelings—sad, but unable to cry. Ironically, I found it beneficial to *discon*nect in order to *reconnect*.

For the most part, our family's feelings of separation in the months surrounding my mother's death were unpleasant—feelings of loss, alienation, loneliness, and disorientation on the part of my mother and on the part of those around her.

Mom's sense of isolation and intense need for connection began a few years before her death, as she searched for the people and the environment she wanted around her in her final days. She seemed unable to settle in a place that provided everything she desired. Even being near my sister proved insufficient, as Mom bemoaned feeling imprisoned in her senior residence. Exacerbating that social isolation was the steady erosion of her physical and mental faculties. Mom's decreased mobility and her increasing difficulty in expressing herself furthered her sense of isolation.

As painful as Mom's death was, our sense of loss didn't begin there. As adult children tending to the needs of a parent with diminishing capacities, our loss began when the dependencies flipped. "Parenting" our parent implied that the true parent was no longer that icon of support and protection. In that sense, it felt as if our parent was already gone—certainly that role had faded away. As an adult child/caregiver, I experienced an incipient sense of being an orphan. Mom, too, may have begun to mourn the loss of her role as provider and nurturer. Each time we would help her prepare for sleep, each time we would leave her behind as we quietly exited her room, my sister and I had that sense that we were the parents putting our child to bed. But the satisfaction that a parent would feel was replaced by increasing sadness.

As siblings living hundreds, and in the case of Jeff, thousands of miles apart, our *physical* separation posed challenges. For one thing, the primary burden of caregiving was on Muff. When Mom had a medical episode, it was Muff at her side. We did connect by phone and occasionally gathered together in person. That usually helped, but there were also emotional divides that were harder to overcome. A big schism between Jeff and me erupted as mourning rituals were compromised and thrown into confusion after 9/11.

After the loss of a loved one, I have often felt a profound sense of separation, not only from the departed, but also from virtually every other person who is not experiencing that loss. Many people, out of fear or ignorance, find it difficult even to speak to someone in mourning. Others lack the empathy to provide support. When Mom died, the world around us was so filled with grief over 9/11 that the loss of a single aging parent seemed trivial in comparison. Being surrounded by people who could not see into my world made me feel that much lonelier in my loss.

1

Tuesday, September 11

OUR DAY STARTS AT *a quarter to six with a call from Jake. At his direction, we turn on the TV to see the World Trade Center's North Tower smoldering. Minutes later, the South Tower is struck. Bit by bit, the events unfold. The Pentagon attack. The South Tower collapse. A fourth plane down in Pennsylvania. The North Tower collapse. Like the rest of the world, we are horrified and transfixed. I feel the need to be informed, to witness the day—a CNN day. At the same time, I feel the need to extricate myself from world events to tend to my already burdened soul. I talk to our rabbi, Nat Ezray. I wonder aloud: "What should I do?" He advises me to take care of myself, to meditate, to write. After hours of staring at televised reports, I force myself out the door and head for my refuge, the baylands. Once there, the beauty and imperturbable essence of the natural environment give me great comfort.*

The baylands is the right place to be two days after Mom's death. Meditating and writing poetry is the right thing to do when our plans for getting her and ourselves to her final resting place have vaporized along with the twin towers.

As the day progresses, I live in a disturbing counterpoint between absorbing the attack and adjusting the logistics of Mom's funeral. Only yesterday, I was walking the streets of San Francisco when Alan called. We discussed funeral plans and travel arrangements. He told me that he, Muff, and Adam were all booked to fly today. I told him that Debbie, Becca, Shira, and I were booked for Wednesday. After literally months of anticipating and discussing plans for Mom's inevitable funeral, I commented

5

to Alan that it seemed that everything was neatly falling into place. As the Yiddish expression goes, "Der mentsh trakht un Got lakht—Man plans, and God laughs."

Today's been a day with more questions than answers. All U.S. flights are grounded. What will transpire in the days ahead is less certain. Is there any chance of a funeral on Thursday? If not, what will happen to my four non-exchangeable, non-refundable airplane tickets? Can we manage to have a funeral in Columbia and get back in time for shiva *(mourning period) in Palo Alto before Rosh Hashanah next Monday evening? There are so many possible scenarios. It's hard to even know what questions to ask. Everything depends on so many unknowns.*

In the evening, Becca and I attend a memorial service—a gathering of four area synagogues. It is a moving program of poetry and song, an opportunity for community grieving. An elder from our temple offers me condolences. I try to describe the struggle I feel juxtaposing my personal grief with this unfathomable tragedy. He means no harm in his response. It comes out wrong, though, when he suggests that Mom's passing is insignificant in the face of the death and destruction rendered by the terrorists. I offer that my grief is not insignificant, just different.

Without today's horror, a mother's death alone would provide ample opportunity for grief and reflection, amidst yearnings for connection, forgiveness, and peace. Under normal circumstances, this would be a very emotional time. How much more so when the entire world around me is suffering and can offer little solace. Now, everything has blown up in our faces. Any illusion about the strength and security of the previously impenetrable United States of America is shattered. Thousands of innocent lives have been lost. And Mom is dead.

A SIMPLE REQUEST

A simple request—
can I just mourn my mother's passing?
The blessing of her life
bombarded by this day of
death and
destruction.

Where does a small mitzvah of mourning go?
When airplanes crash tall buildings
grounding our plans

grounding the deceased
on the wrong coast.
The machinations of evil
colliding with our simple plan
to transport
to bury
to mourn.

Where does a child's grief go?
when the world is draped
with fear, horror,
suffering, sadness.

Is there room for my Kaddish
amidst the wailing cry of humanity?
or
is today a day like every day?
and is one man's grief no greater or smaller
this day than on any other
in the eternal continuum
of good and evil.

DEATH AND A LIFE

When a loved one dies, feelings of separation may extend beyond the loss of that one person. One may feel isolated from the living, as well—from family, friends, and/or community members who are not sharing one's unique experience. In 1974, when my father died on the operating table during open-heart surgery, I was twenty-seven years old and in the midst of my third semester of architecture school. In the wake of this sudden loss, my feelings of estrangement extended to the entire world around me. I took leave from school for a few weeks, first to attend my father's funeral in Columbia, South Carolina, and then to support my mother at her home in Saint Simons Island, Georgia. When I resumed my studies, I remember walking the few short blocks from our apartment to the architecture building as if in a dream. It was incomprehensible to me that I was the only one around who knew that my father had died. I marveled at how everybody else was going along with their business as usual. Of course, that was no dream. It's exactly the way it was.

My journal from September 11, 2001 demonstrates how my alienation seemed amplified by the country's collective shock and grief. Perhaps it was really not so different from my experience after my father's death. In both cases, everyone around me was dealing with their own stuff. Grief, even while in the company of others, can feel very lonely.

The tragedy of 9/11 was marked by its violence, hatred, the sheer number of casualties, and the horror of millions of viewers witnessing it live on television. Mom's death, two days prior to our national trauma, was different in most respects. She had been showered with love throughout her decline, culminating with her slipping away all but unnoticed under cover of night.

Often lost in the magnitude of 9/11 are the individual deaths and their impact on the loved ones of the deceased. Every death is a story of a person, a family, a life—no longer connected on the physical plane, separated suddenly and forever.

THE STORY OF MY Mom's death cannot be fully appreciated without some description of the life that preceded it. Mom's final months were challenging, in stark contrast to her vibrant and productive better times.

Jean Hagar Hymson was born to Charlie and Ida Hymson in Savannah, Georgia on May 18, 1917. She was the third of their four children—the only girl. She was an artistic, vivacious, and often outrageous person throughout her life.

Charlie was a hard-luck but fun-loving businessman, bouncing from one venture to the next, for many years in Louisville, Kentucky. During the Great Depression, Charlie sought greener pastures in Thomasville, Georgia, taking Ida and the two younger children, Jean and Junie, with him, and leaving the two older boys, Morton and Herschel (Bubba), to fend for themselves in Louisville. In 1937, the four in Thomasville moved to Columbia, South Carolina. Columbia became a permanent home for Charlie and Ida. Morton and Bubba eventually joined them. Ida, a homemaker, lived there independently for twenty-four years after Charlie's death in 1951.

When they arrived in Columbia, Jean and Junie were just under twenty and eighteen years of age respectively. At the time, young Jewish women were scarce in Columbia, making Jean a very eligible and attractive prospect for marriage. She was pursued by several of the local Jewish bachelors, as Ida's diaries attest. In the fall of 1939, Sidney Ballon, a young, scholarly rabbi, arrived to lead the Reform Jewish Tree of Life Congregation. From Mom's telling of it, she was serving punch at the temple's welcoming reception and was immediately attracted to this handsome, well-mannered man. Ever the free spirit, she gleefully told us—when we were of age to hear such things—that as soon as she saw Dad she wondered what it would be like to get in the sack with a rabbi! They were married the following summer, which no doubt surprised all who knew of her wilder side.

Jean Hagar Hymson, 1937

Jean and Sidney Ballon, Columbia, South Carolina, c.1940

Throughout their marriage, Mom rarely held a paying job. She preferred to focus on volunteering countless hours in her community, working on myriad art and craft projects, creating a warm home environment centered on her kitchen, and being a true partner and support to her husband. She worked very hard at all of this, preferring volunteerism to being in the paid workforce. She would proclaim that she liked being "good for nothing," not in the conventional sense, but joking that the good she did she provided *gratis*. At a luncheon honoring Mom in 1974, her close friend and fellow *rebbetzin* (rabbi's wife) Marcia Saperstein said:

> . . . Jean anticipated the next stage of the Women's Lib Movement. She has the inner strength, the resourcefulness, to stay home not out of necessity or frustration, but because she knowingly made this choice and made this choice a creative career.

The young couple's life in Columbia was interrupted by the outbreak of World War II. Dad enlisted as a chaplain in the Army Air Corps, and they soon relocated to Keesler Air Force Base in Biloxi, Mississippi, where their first child, Jeff, was born. When Dad was deployed to North Africa, Mom moved back to Columbia for the duration of the war. Muff and I were born in Columbia. In early 1948, the family moved to Lexington, Kentucky, where Mom had some cousins. Then, at the end of 1951, to be closer to Dad's family, and to Mom's chagrin, they settled in West Hempstead, Long Island, New York. For over twenty years, the major pulpit of my father's rabbinate was there at the Nassau Community Temple. In 1974, two years after he had had a heart attack, Mom and Dad felt it was time to leave the harsh winters and metropolitan rat race. Dad took a semi-retirement pulpit at Temple Beth Tefilloh in the small coastal city of Brunswick, Georgia. This congregation, that dates back to 1886, had few daily demands of their rabbi and held only bi-weekly Sabbath services. They resided on Saint Simons Island, a lovely resort area just over the causeway from Brunswick.

Lexington, Kentucky, 1949

**Standing before the *sukkah* in the Nassau Community Temple,
West Hempstead, New York, c.1953**

Unfortunately, Dad's cardiac problems recurred. He went to Dr. Denton Cooley of Houston, one of the world's leading cardiologists and a pioneer in the burgeoning technology of by-pass surgery. Cooley took one look at Dad's deteriorating condition and immediately scheduled surgery. The by-pass itself was successful, but a valve failed and Dad died on the operating table at age sixty-two.

With his death coming less than three months after migrating to the South, some folks wondered whether Mom would move back to New York where she had left behind so many friends and family. I doubt she considered it for a moment. She felt she had been "held hostage" in the north for all those years and was relieved to be back "home" in Georgia. Even alone, she would be happier to build a new life there than to return north.

Moreover, in her short time in Brunswick and Saint Simons, Mom had already gotten involved with many people and activities that would enrich her life there for decades. If she had to move on in life without Dad, this was surely a place where she could do it with panache. With arts and crafts, synagogue, community theater, a close circle of friends, and walks along the beach, Mom truly thrived on Saint Simons Island.

Jean, Saint Simons Island, c. 1980

In 1999, at eighty-two years of age, and anticipating the need to be near family in her waning years, Mom decided to sell her condo on Saint Simons Island and move to Columbia, where she had begun her family over half a century before. She chose Columbia because she had fond memories of her earlier life there, and to be near to her older brother Bubba, and especially his daughter, Linda Hymson George, with whom Mom had a close relationship.

Sadly, but not surprisingly, at least in retrospect, the move did not meet Mom's overly optimistic set of expectations. Suddenly thrust into this new, "old" environment, Mom missed her regular crowd, her familiar stomping grounds, and the engaging activities that had been part of her life on Saint Simons. She could scarcely recognize Columbia from how she remembered it when she was a young adult. Its size was overwhelming. She wasn't comfortable transporting herself about town. Old friends, whom Mom thought would be there for her, were not as present as she had hoped.

The family in Columbia provided some companionship. She would often join them for daily "happy hours" and family gatherings at the home of Linda and her husband, Mike. Linda remained supportive, and saw her Aunt Jean often. But with a full-time job, her own ailing parents, two growing boys, and a household to maintain, Linda's very full life put constraints on what she could provide for Mom. Moreover, Bubba had just been diagnosed with dementia, probably from Alzheimer's, which seemed to have contributed to a less than satisfactory relationship with his sister.

After about a year, disillusioned, Mom headed back to Saint Simons Island. But even that fell short of expectations. In her absence, her friends had adapted to new social patterns that did not mesh with Mom's needs and desires. For a while, she tried to make it work. But in 2000, she took a major leap across the country to move near Muff in Riverside, California. It seemed a desperate search for connection.

2

Wednesday, September 12

AFTER MONTHS OF TEDIOUS, *sometimes challenging, and even a little argumentative planning of what we would be doing at the inevitable event of our mother's death, the most fundamental logistics are a mess. With the attack, air travel has been suspended, and transportation to Columbia is stalled, including the shipment of Mom's body. We manage to eke out some information. After our flight is canceled, we learn that our plane tickets are refundable. One less concern.*

The larger issues, for our family at least—where, when, how to mourn—are still shrouded in confusion. What do we do at the ritual level? Jewish practice is to bury the dead as quickly as possible, typically within three days, and then to enter a week of mourning immediately after the funeral. But we don't know when that will happen.

The answer to this comes in a surprising and infuriating manner. Despite months of collaboration, Jeff calls from Florida and tells me after the fact that he unilaterally conducted a shiva minyan *in his household this evening! What??!! I listen to his reasoning. He says that Jewish law provides that in time of war, when a body cannot be returned, the family is to start the ritual mourning immediately, rather than after interment.*

Still, I'm perplexed. Is this a war? Isn't there at least a chance that we'll see some flights going out this week and have a funeral soon? I think he's jumping the gun. The attacks were only yesterday and all the facts are not in. But more important, and quite galling, is that he has acted on his own after we had worked so long and hard to achieve consensus about Mom's arrangements. Why not a phone call earlier in the day? Why not work in concert with his siblings? Was he trying to beat us to the punch by forging ahead without us?

Our collective response to 9/11 is now one of confusion, resentment, and anger. That's sometimes what happens around life-cycle events, even under the best of circumstances—they open a floodgate of old wounds and emotions. Our national tragedy has really messed up the time-honored mourning process. It's challenging enough to mourn Mom's loss amidst the turmoil of the nation. This lack of unity among the family does nothing to ameliorate that.

That said, with Jeff's announcement, I feel the train has left the station and I need to get on board. I call the rabbi and ask if he would like to take a walk with me tomorrow—something we've done several times during Mom's decline.

UNRAVELING

Separation does not always occur in a defined moment. However, if there is one event that could somehow mark the beginning of the end for Mom, it would be Passover 2001. Almost the entire clan had gathered for seder at my sister's house in Riverside. There were already whispers that this might be "Granny's Last Hurrah." Mom—Granny to the next generation—seemed to be mustering every bit of energy and resolve to overcome whatever ills she had been suffering during her long days at Villa De Anza, the independent residence where she was to endure her final months on the planet.

Mom had been diagnosed with Parkinson's disease. The accuracy of the diagnosis was in doubt. Regardless, the aches and pains of being eighty-four years of age, her diminishing sense of balance that had led to occasional falls, and maybe just the feelings of confinement living in a senior residence clearly set her on a path to the finish line.

Thus, we were all the more delighted that she was having a day where her indomitable spirit was rising to the occasion. It was the Mom/Granny of old, pitching in to create the festival meal, singing, joking, laughing, and making her trademark wise-ass remarks.

We gathered for a portrait in Muff's living room to commemorate the occasion. Jeff and Ann Lois had been in China not long before, so Mom held a souvenir photo of them in ceremonial garb as a way of including them in the picture.

**Standing, left to right: Doug (Yesh), Debbie, Muff, Alan. Kneeling: Adam, Josh, Jake.
Seated: Becca, Shira, Mom, Sara. Passover 2001**

As lovely as Passover was, and as strong as Mom seemed, the unravel-
ing proceeded shortly thereafter. A week or so later, she fell again. She was
bruised, pulled apart, and sewn back together. She lay in a bed, far from my
home and far from the home she had known for a quarter of a century. She
was paying the price of becoming bi-coastal.

Not only was I frustrated by the physical distance between me and
Mom, at times I felt removed from what was going on inside myself. I would
hear my sister's stories—how much it took for her to see Mom through a
long night in the E.R. But how little I could do from Palo Alto! It was even
hard for me to shed a tear.

As inaccessible as my emotions were to me, the rabbi knew—how he
knew!—from the smallest catch in my throat I thought imperceptible. Or
did he know even before that? When I sat with him to unload my concerns,
he peered inside my soul further than I had dared look myself. It was his
knowing glance, his words of care that let me know there was so much more
to feel. It made me wonder—what if I just said it? What if I opened my
journal and wrote, "My mom is dying, a slow, ambiguous death, and I don't
know whether to pray for recovery or demise." Then I learned to pray for
healing—that it was not for me to choose; it was for her to become whole,
however that might look.

WITH MOTHER'S DAY APPROACHING, I devised a plan to join my brother
and sister to celebrate with Mom. That Sunday morning, I would fly from
San Jose to Ontario—near Riverside—rent a car, hang with them for the
day, crash at Muff's place, then drive to San Diego the next day for business.
But the trip took on larger proportions when Mom fell yet again—this time
landing in the emergency room with a dislocated shoulder and stitches on
her head.

After that fall, Mom did not go back to Villa De Anza immediately. She
was checked into a rehab facility, hoping that with proper medication and
some therapy, she could regain enough of her wellbeing to return to independent living in her apartment. Muff and I talked about this at length one
day. When my phone rang the next night and I recognized Muff's voice on
the line, I knew right away that she couldn't be calling with good news. After
a couple of weeks there, the rehab center had given us only three days to take
Mom someplace else. Apparently, she had made some physical progress, but
her mental condition had deteriorated to the point where they didn't feel
she had the capacity to benefit from physical therapy. She was hallucinating.
Her memory was poor. She didn't really know where she was. It was back to
Villa De Anza for her, at least for the time being.

So, I moved up my reservation and flew down to Southern California
on the Friday before Mother's Day. Muff and I planned to reevaluate Mom's
living arrangements before Jeff's arrival on Saturday. Mostly, I was there just
to be there. We had no idea what would transpire. Three kids doing the best
we could to help our mom live or die with as much comfort and dignity that
the system, our hearts, and our purses could muster.

After my arrival, our immediate plan was to pick up some medicine
at Rite-Aid, drop me off at Mom's while Muff had her hair done, then take
Mom back to Muff's for Shabbat dinner. The stop at Rite-Aid was another
manifestation of alienation—a study in the frustrations that many people
face trying to get healthcare, especially after having changed insurers. It
was the kind of service I have sadly come to expect from a computerized
pharmaceutical conglomerate—the kind of impersonal exchange that was
unimaginable when as kids we could wander into Doc Roochvarg's drug-
store and be truly cared for. Muff had many tales of similar frustrations
and miscommunications that she had suffered dealing with various agen-
cies and providers, and that was all beside dealing with Mom herself! It's a
wonder how she withstood the ordeal.

Muff dropped me off at Villa De Anza—a fairly pleasant residence,
clean, and staffed by enthusiastic, caring young people. I scanned the dining
room to see if Mom was at her table for lunch. She was not. I greeted some of
the residents sitting in the lobby, and proceeded down the cigarette-scented

hallway to Mom's apartment. When I arrived, she was all dressed and seated expectantly in her living room. Most of the bruises on her face and the cut on her nose were healed. She didn't look much different than when I last saw her at Passover. She had been in great spirits then. She had put on a pretty good show.

This day, however, her first words were: "Just throw me away."

Even with occasional pauses, I had no difficulty making conversation with Mom. I had little to offer her, but she never sat for more than a few moments without commenting on something. She showed me the bruises on her legs. She struggled to remember the name of her housekeeper—Stella—who told her some food was rotting in the mini-fridge.

Mom didn't believe there was anything wrong with her shoulder, but just for appearances, she would wear the sling that was prescribed. Meanwhile, the sling was nowhere in sight. She accused every one of her service providers of being money-grubbing— a thought that never would have occurred to her in her healthy, free-spending days.

Jeff called. The two of them chatted a bit. Then Mom handed the phone to me. Jeff commented that this was going to be a hard trip. I concurred. I had been thinking that all week. Whenever I mentioned to someone where and why I would be traveling that weekend, I'd felt an urge to cry. From a distance, it seemed so large and grievous. Now that I was there, it seemed small and tedious.

I asked Mom if she was meditating at all. I had given her some instructions on a previous visit. In a desperate tone, she said she didn't want to deal with anything technical. I wasn't sure what she meant by that. Then, she rattled off a long list of "technical" issues that she found annoying. "Physical therapy—that's technical. Relaxation—that's technical. Going to the bathroom—that's technical. Wiping my butt—that's technical."

She didn't want any more techniques for anything and made that amply clear. Okay!

I looked around the room at pictures of the family from when we were all much younger. I tried to reconcile the memories that the photos evoked with the person sitting before me—and I couldn't.

Muff arrived with In-n-Out burgers. The first thing she did was put Mom's sling on her. We ate, then went through one of those tedious techniques—putting her in the wheelchair. We headed down the hall—a long, carpeted stretch. Her unit was at the extreme end of her wing. Mom commented on how much shorter the hall seemed when traversed by wheelchair rather than by her feeble legs. Walking the corridor was no longer within her capabilities.

We transferred Mom to the car, left the wheelchair by the De Anza main entrance, and headed off to Muff's. Mom didn't have the use of one arm, so upon our arrival, she was forced to use a one-handed walker to assist her from the vehicle to Muff's front door. Thirty feet over the uneven ground seemed like a mile, but she persevered. Once inside, she barreled right down the hall to a bedroom, whereupon she took a long nap.

We had a quiet Shabbat dinner. Mom had eaten only a half of a hamburger at lunch, so before dinner she snacked on a bowl of Chex-mix. Consequently, she ate little of her dinner and was not even tempted by dessert, which ordinarily she would not have missed. Before long, it was time to begin the protracted return trek—the slow walk to the car, the drive across town to Villa De Anza, and then the wheelchair ride down the long corridor to her apartment. I absented myself while Muff got Mom into her nightclothes. Mom was in bed by quarter to nine.

Soon, we were joined by a very sweet aide who brought medications and a portable commode. Neither Muff nor I anticipated a very positive response from Mom on the arrival of yet another piece of equipment meant for a debilitated person. But perhaps the timing helped. Mom had just managed to get herself into bed, and was no doubt unhappy about the prospect of having to make her way to the bathroom. In any case she was thrilled to see the commode. I couldn't decide if her acceptance was a good thing or bad. In truth, it was both.

Muff and I kissed Mom goodnight, closed the apartment door behind us, and headed down the corridor with a familiar emotional tug.

ALWAYS A FOOD FEST

The meager appetite Mom displayed in those days lay in stark contrast to her prior life as a foodie—yet another manifestation of separation from life as it once was. In her prime, there may have been no topic of greater interest to her than food. She loved to prepare it, serve it, consume it, talk about it. We were continuously embraced by her love of food.

My Southern/Jewish mother was acknowledged by many to be a master in the kitchen. This was especially true in the era before cholesterol became the enemy. Many of her dishes were so tasty, if for no other reason than she seemed to throw a stick of butter in the frying pan before even deciding on the menu. Approaching home after a long day of school, the smell of onions sautéing in butter often hit us well before we reached the front door!

Her signature dish was southern fried chicken. She doted over each piece sizzling in her cast iron pan, turning constantly, lovingly, browning to perfection. Also, no one anywhere, anytime ever made a moister, more flavorful Thanksgiving turkey, with its succulent gravy flavored with onions, celery, white wine, and orange juice—and again, plenty of butter!

Mom had all the traditional Ashkenazi Jewish dishes down to perfection as well—matzoh ball soup, tzimmes, potato kugel, potato latkes, cheese blintzes, chopped liver, honey cake, hamentashen with her unique brown sugar dough, rugelach before it was trendy . . . the list goes on. She was a prolific baker and would support community events by cranking out hundreds of pieces of dessert in assembly-line fashion.

Mom's focus on food was so profound that she took it upon herself to gather recipes, mostly from women in the temple sisterhood, as well as from some family and friends, and edit not one, but two cookbooks.

3

Thursday, September 13

THE RABBI MEETS ME *at the baylands with one-year-old Ethan in the stroller. It is naptime for Ethan, but the excitement of the waterfowl keeps him alert and awake. Nat and I talk about the terrorist attacks for a while before we get into the subject of mourning rituals. Jewish law in this regard is fairly clear about what to do and when to do it.*

First, there is the time between death and burial. This is called aninut, *an interim period, usually a day or two, during which the family has but one duty: to prepare for the* mitzvah *(commandment, spiritual obligation good deed) of burying their dead. Shiva, the seven-day mourning period, commences immediately after burial. It provides a powerfully therapeutic structure to deal with the loss of a close relative. Four days after Mom's death, with no notion of when a funeral will occur, this extended period of* aninut *has become particularly uncomfortable.*

With regard to proceeding with shiva *before interment—as Jeff has done—Nat says that he had already been contemplating taking the same approach. As we are walking and talking, my cell phone rings. Alan confirms that there is no way Mom will be shipped east by air before Monday. The mortuary will look into rail as an alternative. With that news, and Nat's support, my decision is made. We will start* shiva *tonight. Though uncertainty about Mom's funeral lingers, at least with* shiva *commencing, we will gain some measure of comfort.*

When I get home, I call Muff to let her know my intention. She is okay with it. She and Alan will fly up to join the family in the Bay Area. I call Jeff, who, of course, has already been reciting Kaddish *(mourners' prayer). Naturally, he has no objection to my decision to follow his lead. When I check in with Debbie, she suggests that we keep this first night small—just family and a few close friends. We were all supposed to have been in Columbia for the funeral tonight, anyway, flying back home for* shiva minyanim *on Saturday and Sunday evenings and Monday morning. We had already notified the congregation of these plans, so we don't need to change anything from that perspective. Keeping tonight small puts less stress on all of us.*

Nat tells me he is unavailable to lead tonight's minyan. *I figure we'll do it ourselves. Debbie suggests finding other clergy. This is a wise idea. Rabbi Teitelbaum, our beloved rabbi emeritus, immediately agrees to lead us in prayer.*

It is a beautiful gathering. After conducting the evening service, Rabbi Teitelbaum encourages us to talk about Mom. I read some excerpts from my journals of the summer, including Mom's words about Yiddishkeit *(Jewishness) and a selection from* Pirke Avot *that she and I had talked about. I read my poems "A Healing Poem for the Son" and "A Simple Request." It is very moving and comforting for me to do this. Gene Mielke, the husband of Mom's beloved cousin Myra, reminisces about playing cards with Mom, her matzoh ball soup, and their fondness for "French . . . oops!" He means* Scotch Kisses—*a favorite caramel and marshmallow confection from* See's Candy.

DARK HUMOR

The slow march to Mom's inevitable end was not always a dour experience. My siblings and I were capable of experiencing the full range of emotions. We were raised in a house that knew how to laugh as well as cry—sometimes both at once. When your father is out most Sundays "hitching & ditching" (performing weddings and funerals), it provides some perspective on the ebb and flow of life.

There we were, entering Mother's Day weekend. Muff had been very non-committal with Mom as to when or if we would see her on Saturday. Understandably, Muff was carving out space for a day of rest from the demands of dealing with Mom. I, on the other hand, had come a distance to be with Mom for the weekend. I knew that the Villa was celebrating Mother's Day one day early. There was a special luncheon on Saturday for the predominantly female residents and their families. I couldn't rationalize Mom sitting alone in her room while many of the other "inmates," as she called them, were joined by their loved ones. Consequently, Muff and I went to the luncheon. When we arrived, Mom was already sitting in her wheelchair waiting for her ride down to the dining room. I asked her if she'd like to jog, and so we sped our way down the hall, making it "even shorter."

The buffet was well attended and in full swing. There were pink balloons and roses on the tables, and chrysanthemum corsages for the women. I made a platter for Mom—ham, yams, green beans, baked potatoes. I brought it to her and proceeded to prepare the potato and cut up the ham. She only half-jokingly lamented that although she had always wanted a servant, she now despised depending on others for her care. I reminded her of her own annoying words, often uttered over the years when she did something for one of us: "Someday you'll do something for me." That day had arrived.

We had a pleasant enough time with those at our table—other old women and their adult children. There was plenty of joking and laughing.

As we headed back to Mom's room, we were joined in the elevator by a man visiting his two grandmothers. He had never before been above the ground floor where they lived, but this weekend, he and his wife had taken a guest room on the second floor. He commented that he had been unaware that the building had three floors. Mom, in her delusion, and her customary authoritative manner, explained to him that residents had to be a certain height and weight to live up there. She also told him about the levitating man in her rehab center. Her confusion sounded so funny, and at the same time, not so funny at all.

We put Mom down for her nap, and left.

On our way out, fortuitously, we ran into Lori, the director of the facility, whom Muff knew from previous visits. We talked about Mom's condition and the housing options we were considering. If Mom could not become ambulatory, she would not be allowed by state law to reside above the ground floor—too much risk in the event of an evacuation. I figured that Mom's tangled cerebral connections had caused her to take this fact and distort it into her statement about the height and weight criteria for living upstairs.

Muff and I took advantage of our chance meeting with Lori to check out some available ground-level apartments. The one that made the most sense was a studio with a view of the pond in the back of the property. As Mom's capacities were diminishing, her physical domain was shrinking as well. In her current condition, her one-bedroom apartment was more turf than she could comfortably and safely navigate. We felt she would be a lot better off if everything she needed was closer—not to mention the cost savings that could be applied to the greater amount of care she was requiring.

We also felt it would be a tough sell. Like so many others in her condition, Mom would want to hold on to as many reminders of the past as possible—even if they had become useless, or worse, impediments to her daily living.

Later on, Jeff arrived—too late, really, to visit Mom, but all the siblings were now together. We went out with Alan to a new soul food joint that had gotten a great write-up in the paper. It was an amusing evening. In the previous two days, the family running the restaurant had not been able to cope with the success brought to them by the article. There were four generations there—three of them hard at work. They had long run out of many of their specialties, including the ribs, greens, and banana pudding with 'Nilla wafers and whipped cream. Despite their hapless service, their faces and their attitudes were so sweet. We enjoyed their chatter and they ours, and we stuffed ourselves with all that did finally come out of the kitchen.

Conversation about Mom ran from the tactical to the comical. We all agreed. The studio apartment would work best for her. We thought of drawing straws to see who would tell her. Muff and I had been kidding before his arrival: "Let Jeffie do it!"

ON SUNDAY, WE DECIDED to bring a bagel brunch over to Mom. When we arrived, she was sitting in the living room. She had been waiting there for hours. Just as we began to eat, Jake arrived from Westwood, at least an hour away under the best conditions. This was his second visit to his grandmother in as many weekends. He was a real sport. The previous week, he sat with her for two hours in the rehab center. She was a good deal more beat up and hallucinogenic back then.

Mom was in good spirits through brunch. Then, Jeff led her to the bedroom. He said he wanted to talk business with her. I didn't know what else he was saying. When I walked by the door to her room, he invited me in. Apparently, he had set things up pretty well. When I told Mom what we had learned from Lori, Mom was totally receptive of moving downstairs to the smaller unit. She didn't even flinch when I told her she would have to give up her beloved king-sized bed—perhaps the most visible remnant of her long-past married life.

**Muff, Jeff, Mom, Doug (Yesh), Villa De Anza, Riverside, California,
Mother's Day 2001**

Mom asked us all to stay as she took a nap. It wasn't long before she called out from the bedroom to Muff, who wheeled Mom out into the living room.

Unafraid to engage in a little dark humor, I decided to share with her the "fun" plans that we had been kicking around for marking her eventual demise. Jeff had suggested that we gather the clan at Mom's old Saint Simons Island environs. We would rent a shrimp boat and scatter her ashes at sea, then come ashore for a big party. She seemed enthusiastic. But then, on a more serious note, she asked that we save some ashes to be placed next to Dad's resting place in Columbia—at the gravesite that was reserved for her.

That brought up the whole topic of the ash urn she had commissioned years before, and the humorous sayings she had solicited from us to adorn it. We retrieved the round ceramic vessel that her friend had made. Mom was disappointed with the style, although none of us know what she had expected. Inside the urn were papers on which we had scribbled our suggested rhymes—none of which had been inscribed on the urn. There were gems like, "We couldn't restrain her until we got her in this container."

I was reading them aloud when randomly, one set us off in a fit of laughter: "In this half-gallon is what's left of Jean Ballon." Probably one of those "you-had-to-be-there" situations. Nonetheless, our convulsive laughter was just the cathartic I had been needing for days. The tears finally flowed, even if not from weeping.

Not long after that, Mom was ready for another nap. Perhaps—desperately wanting to be with us—she never really had had the first one. For me, this marked the end of the visit with Mom. I wouldn't be seeing her again that night, and I was heading off to San Diego early the next morning.

We headed back to Muff's to while away the rest of the afternoon. We explored some outstanding issues, such as Mom's finances and when we would implement the move. We gathered information about applying Medi-Cal to board & care facilities.

The big moments and the significant accomplishments of Mother's Day weekend were behind us. We had been present. We had been caring—not just for Mom, but for one another. We had succeeded in gaining consensus on her living arrangements. While Mom's continuous mental and physical slide was a cause for grief, and while we all acknowledged having shed the occasional tear in the days leading to this reunion, I truly believe the most deeply shared moment was that irreverent, raucous, therapeutic laugh.

Muff expressed her appreciation to Jeff and me in a subsequent email:

> Hey—
> I'm sure it meant a lot to Mom for you to be here this weekend, but I need to tell you that it was a real boost for me. I really appreciated your both leaving your families to be here. I'm not sure if I would have handled this weekend very well alone. And I feel like we accomplished a great deal together. Thanks.
>
> I stopped at Mom's this evening on the way home, and as of about 7pm at least, she hadn't fallen today! I am going to try to move at least the bed, a chair, clothes, and the TV in this weekend. That's just to get her in the smaller space. We can deal with the other stuff when you can get here. Lori assured me we can take our time—there is no one waiting for her current apt. Mom is really struggling to understand why she can't just get up and go when she wants!
> love— m

Two weeks later, Muff provided the following update:

> I spent another long day in the ER. Mom had some kind of a seizure last night, and this morning could not even stand without her legs just crumpling beneath her. Again they found nothing— negative x-rays, CT, etc.—no evidence of stroke, aneurysm. The doc appears baffled. He did add an Alzheimer's med to possibly help her mental status. That's all I know.

4

Friday, September 14

TODAY IS MY FIRST *full day of mourning. I take it easy at home. I stay away from news coverage as much as possible, as I have all week. I read some, and continue to communicate with many people by phone and email. While last night's* shiva *provided some comfort, we are still in limbo about plans for the funeral.*

Some clarity arrives when Muff calls to say that the mortuary decided to ship Mom's remains to South Carolina by train. The estimated time of arrival should be in the early hours of Tuesday morning. We joke that if no one meets her train, her coffin will circle the baggage conveyor all night long. It's still not clear when the funeral will be.

In the evening, we have dinner at the home of our friends, the Steins, en route to Shabbat services at synagogue. According to custom, mourners are acknowledged at a certain point in the service with a somewhat archaic but traditional prayer.

Ha-makom y'nakhem etkhem b'tokh sh'ar avelei tziyon virushalayim.
May God comfort you together with all the other mourners of Zion and Jerusalem.

When the congregation recites the prayer, I join in as well because we are not the only mourners tonight. Another family has lost a dad, apparently still a young man raising a family.

YIDDISHKEIT

The middle of the summer of 2001 was filled with unanticipated discoveries. Our interactions with Mom underwent a remarkable transformation. It was preceded by Muff and Alan's visit to the Bay Area the last weekend in July. They had come to attend the Gilroy Garlic Festival and visit their younger son, Adam, as well as to see us. While they were here, Muff presented a letter that Mom's younger brother, Junie, had sent to her. In it, Uncle Junie recounted all the reasons he admired his big sister and showed his appreciation for the blessings he had seen her enjoying in life. The issue for Muff was whether to show it to Mom, and if so, when and how.

After putting her into hospice care, Muff, for whatever reason, had not had a frank conversation with Mom about the assessment that her death was not far off. Debbie and I were of the same mind that this was a conversation that needed to take place before Junie's letter could be dealt with. In addition to shouldering her unrelenting logistical and medical burdens, Muff struggled with communicating with Mom—it often felt like they were talking in two different languages. It was a continuous, losing battle. I told Muff I would be there to assist her or to talk with Mom myself if she preferred.

The turning point came when Debbie, who volunteered as a counselor at Kara, a grief support organization in Palo Alto, gave us a book entitled *Final Gifts: Understanding the Special Awareness, Needs, and Communication of the Dying* by Maggie Callanan and Patricia Kelly. The book, as it turned out, had a marked effect on the weeks that followed.

A few days later, Muff called from Riverside. She had had a profound experience with Mom that evening. Muff had read *Final Gifts,* and discovered a whole new way of listening to Mom's seemingly irrational words. The book helped Muff understand that people who are near death often express themselves allegorically—words that make little literal sense may be filled with figurative meaning. For example, if someone was to say, "I want to go home" when, in fact, they already *were* home, it could be interpreted to mean "I want to die."

For Muff, *Final Gifts* was the Rosetta Stone. Suddenly, she had a decoder to help her receive some message, if not the exact one Mom intended. More importantly, content had become less important than process. Mom might speak in allegories, metaphors, insults, whatever—but now, Muff was free to sense the underlying spiritual/emotional messages, and not worry about understanding her literal words. So instead of confronting or dismissing Mom when she said, "I want to go to an oasis," Muff asked Mom to tell her about the oasis. When Mom asked if Muff would join her, Muff said she would at some time, but not right away. Things opened up for both of them with this new way of listening and responding. For the first time, it seemed they could consider ending the futile struggle. Muff reported that after this conversation, Mom's breathing eased and she seemed much more peaceful.

I knew I had not been fully dealing with Mom's situation. Although I occasionally flew down to Riverside to visit with her, I felt an increasing emotional buildup inside that I hadn't addressed. Debbie suggested that I speak with one of her colleagues who volunteered with her at Kara. So the day after hearing from Muff about her breakthrough with Mom, I had lunch with Ken.

Ken, too, was dealing with his mother's impending death. At lunch, he told me that he was flying to Kansas City every other week for a long weekend, to spend time with his mom. Once, he stayed there for a whole week and he felt that was especially valuable. Sometimes he would visit his mom alone, sometimes with his wife at his side. Each visit provided a different kind of experience with different insights. I left lunch convinced that I wanted to go down to Riverside as soon as I could.

When I returned to my office, I immediately called Muff to check in with her before making plans. Literally as I was dialing her, my cell phone rang. It was she. She had just left Mom. They had had another conversation. They dealt frankly with death. Muff read her Junie's letter. At first, Mom, in typical fashion, made some dismissive remark. By the time Muff got to the end of the letter, however, Mom was acknowledging how sweet it was.

When they talked about death, Mom said, "Maybe next Tuesday would be a good time."

Muff said that the *Final Gifts* book describes similar situations where people actually predict or choose the time of their deaths. Mom was not suffering from an immediate physical threat to her survival. Still, we had to take seriously the possibility that her psychological or spiritual state could lead her to dying on Tuesday. This was a Friday. I booked seats for Debbie and me on Southwest Airlines for the very next day.

SATURDAY, AUGUST 4, 2001, was a day I'll never forget. In the afternoon, the tenor of our conversation with Mom took us all by surprise—perhaps Muff the most, because she had been at Mom's side so much without having ever heard such an outpouring. Had we known we would be in for such a treat, perhaps we would have taped it. Only after it became apparent that we were witness to this one-woman show—"the world according to Mom"—did I pick up my pen and start scribbling down some of her words as best I could.

There was a sweetness in Mom's expression, her every word. There was a childlike innocence, a simplicity; and at the same time, a mystical wisdom.

Many of her words were difficult to hear or interpret, and we tried to clarify as much as we could. Sometimes, the images and metaphors she spoke were elegant yet undecipherable—at other times, explicitly clear. *Final Gifts* presents some common themes that people nearing death often mention. Two of them were very present in Mom's afternoon chatter: traveling and religion.

She spoke at length about "*Yiddishkeit*." It may have started when she used a Yiddish expression, "*Morgn iz an ander tog*—Tomorrow is another day," marveling at the beauty of Yiddish. She told me a story, perhaps from her childhood, perhaps from her medicated imagination, about having once, in an effort to eliminate Judaism from her life, cut to pieces a telephone book of Jewish names. Or was it a prayer book? Or both? Or neither? I didn't know what to believe.

She seemed to make a play on words, indicating that *Jewish* was *joyous*, sadly noting that some people shun things "Jewish" while others surround themselves with things "joyous." She acknowledged shocking everyone by marrying a rabbi. She expressed a clear love of the *Yiddishkeit* she had lived. *Yiddishkeit!*—a word we may never have heard her utter before, now actually spoken with reverence.

She also spoke of taking trips—imaginary trips—on trains and planes. I told her I had just had a vivid dream with planes and trains. I described the image of a military jet soaring straight up into the sky. She responded by saying that that was how one succeeded, by going straight up. Later, she said of her train trip, "If I don't go, the kids won't go. I always take the children with me."

Muff then suggested that perhaps this time she would go without them for now.

At one point, perhaps because I had mentioned my dream, Mom started talking about dreams—having dreams in one's life. She seemed captivated by the thought of *unthinkable dreams*. She was proud of having lived them.

> The unthinkable dream—you have to dream it yourself. No one else can dream it for you . . . You don't have to be on the train to dream it. It's unthinkable until you get someone to help you . . . then it becomes thinkable. . . . Just say, "I need help." . . . It's a lovely dream. You just have to think far enough ahead. . . . We can always move around in our dreams or in reality. . . . Take someone you know and impose this thought on them, or take someone you don't know and impose this thought on them. . . . If this doesn't work, look for an answer another way.

As I continue to unravel the underlying meaning of Mom's unusual utterances, I wonder if when she said, "I always take the children with me," it might have been a reflection of her sense of responsibility to pass her heritage on *l'dor vador*, from generation to generation. At the same time, she didn't believe in "doing Jewish" in one exclusive way. Her words "you have to dream it yourself" convey to me the notion that we must pay attention to our own dreams, not those imposed by others. "You don't have to be on the train" not only reflects the possibility of forging one's own path, but also reminds us to not be in a hurry. And when we want the company of others, we can just say, "I need help," thereby building meaningful and lasting relationships. *How* Mom lived her Judaism was far less important than that she lived it *fully*, with true love and devotion.

Mom later managed to combine the topics of traveling and religion. "There's a beautiful story about imaginary trips at the end of the *Pirke Avot*."

Pirke Avot, sometimes translated as *Ethics of the Fathers,* is a collection of maxims. In my youth, I watched Mom regularly turn to it in the prayer book as we were waiting for Shabbat services to begin, or during silent devotion. Since she had mentioned it, that evening I opened a copy of the latest Reform Jewish prayer book, *Gates of Prayer*, which would have been Mom's most likely source. Their abridged *Pirke Avot* ends with a passage that tells of the conversation between two travelers meeting on the road. One, a rabbi, concludes his remarks by saying:

> . . . when we die it is neither silver nor gold nor gems nor pearls that accompany us, but Torah and good deeds only.
> —Pirke Avot 6:9

Mom's surprising display of *Yiddishkeit* had me thinking that perhaps she would find it meaningful to include some Jewish ritual as part of her dying process. I called my friend Alison, a nurse and therapist, who had done a lot of work both physically and spiritually with dying patients. She had been studying the Jewish deathbed confessional—the *Vidui*. I knew little about it, but I figured this might be the time to learn more. Alison and I talked about Mom's startling outpouring. Alison told me that the Reform Jewish liturgy had a translation of the *Vidui* that might be more meaningful for Mom than a more literal, traditional translation. I decided this was something I was ready to pursue. I hit the Internet and searched for whatever I could find about the *Vidui*. There was some information, but I couldn't find the prayer itself. I did confirm, as Alison had mentioned, that it could be found in the Reform movement's *Gates of Home* prayer book.

ON MONDAY, MUFF LEFT very early for work. I arose, taking myself for a morning walking meditation—a "walk 'n' talk," as I call it—during which I prayed for guidance so I could be of the greatest assistance to Mom. Then, I headed to Villa De Anza. The Reform congregation in Riverside was en route. I made that my first stop. I walked into the office and asked if the rabbi were available. My primary mission was to get a copy of the *Vidui*. I also wondered if Mom would be interested in talking with a rabbi or having the rabbi lead her in reciting this prayer.

The office administrator was quick to let me know that the rabbi wasn't really available; he had just arrived in town and had not officially started the job. Then she added that if it was urgent, she would see if he'd be available to talk with me. I said it was rather urgent. By this time, the thought of personally getting some support from a rabbi was sounding good for my own benefit, as well as Mom's.

While waiting, I decided to look in the library for the *Vidui*. I asked where the library was and learned that the paltry shelves around me constituted the library. It only took a few minutes to find the prayer, and the administrator obligingly made a copy for me. I continued to peruse the bookshelves and found myself getting increasingly emotional at the thought of meeting with a rabbi. I felt I might burst into tears at the first opportunity.

Soon, a man who had been in the room the entire time finished his phone call. The administrator addressed him as Rabbi, and asked him if he was able to spend some time with me.

The rabbi took me back to a bare, windowless office. He was literally just moving in, and was unhappy that the moving van was six hours late. When I introduced myself, he immediately engaged in "Jewish Geography," asking if I was related to a Reform rabbi in Florida with the same last name. We spent a few minutes chatting about Jeff. Already, I felt my emotional distress . . . not waning, so much, as heading back down for cover. As the conversation wore on, I heard more about his concerns than he heard of mine—his new pulpit, the van, a recent divorce. This was not what I came in for. He was undergoing a lot, and I was in a forgiving mood—after all, I wasn't even one of his congregants. I was satisfied to make it out of there, *Vidui* in hand. I also decided that I wouldn't be asking Mom if she wanted to talk with a rabbi.

5

Saturday, September 15

THIS MORNING IS THE *bat mitzvah of Elana Weil. I don't know her too well, but years ago, I worked with her mom, Adrienne, on the committee that selected and hired the rabbi. I am happy to celebrate this* simcha *(joyous occasion) with them. Elana shows immense maturity and intellect as she probes the meaning of her Torah portion. The only thing missing is her father, David. He has been traveling for business, and was stranded in Europe when international flights were suspended following the attacks. But what we in the pews don't realize, until Nat tells us midway through the service, is that David is attending via telephone. He is listening to every word. He even speaks to his daughter and the entire congregation.*

There is a poignancy and a connection to history provided by David's absence. He points out how lucky they are knowing he will be home soon, how much more aware their family is of the preciousness of life and of not taking anything for granted. Even a tragedy has its blessings.

Earlier in the week, Nat asked me if he could use my poem "A Simple Request" in his Shabbat sermon. He wanted to demonstrate the effect the attacks are having on everyday life. During the service, Nat comes over to me and asks me if I will read the poem myself. I oblige. When he comes to that point in his remarks, he tells the congregation what our family is going through. I ascend the bimah *(raised platform) and, not without some emotion, read the poem. The juxtaposition of my plight with the bat mitzvah father's remarks is deeply felt by those present.*

After the service, I ask Nat if it is appropriate for me to stay for the kiddush *(celebratory luncheon). He said it is, I suppose because there is no public mourning on Shabbat. During* kiddush, *one congregant comes over to me to talk about the poem, and bursts into tears. It no doubt has touched a raw nerve, as her son has just announced that instead of going to college, he plans to enlist in the Army. I find myself on the giving end of consolation.*

Tonight is our first minyan *with the larger community. Close to thirty people gather in our living room. For me, this is one of the most powerful experiences as a Jew—to be comforted and supported by others, to hear their voices rise as one within the modest confines of our home. A family friend from our childhood sings* Esa Einai, *a passage from Psalm 121, in her beautiful mezzo soprano voice.*

Esa einai el heharim,
Me'ayin, me'ayin yavo ezri?
Ezri me'im Adonai,
Oseh shamayim va'aretz.

I lift my eyes to the mountain.
From where will my help come?
My help comes from God,
Maker of heaven and earth.

After Kaddish, *I tell the group how grateful I am for their presence. A few others make some comments. I read some of the same writings about Mom that I had shared with the smaller group last night.*

YEARNING

After picking up the copy of the *Vidui*, I spent the day with Mom at Villa De Anza. That afternoon, she asked me to help her with a lamp—an imaginary one. She did not know how to work it.

I asked, "Do you want me to turn out the light?"

"Yes!"

"Shall we both work on it?"

"Yes . . . alone."

"Do you want to be alone, or with me?"

"With you."

"When shall we do it?"

"Anytime. What time is it now?"

"It's twenty minutes to five. Let's wait until after Muff is here,"

"Okay. That will give me a chance for a nap."

Muff arrived after work. At 6:18 p.m., Mom said she'd like to go to sleep in half an hour. Considering the possibility that Mom was revising the "forecast" of her death, Muff sat on the edge of the bed holding her hand, weeping softly. I sat in an armchair facing them, meditating on *shalom*, channeling my energy of peace in their direction. For all we knew, Mom would be gone at 6:48. This did not come to pass. Mom spoke: "There's Grandma and Grandpa and there's you and Jeff and each of you has a little bit. . . . A piece of that is home? What are you going to do about it?"

Muff asked Mom, "Do you want to go home?"

"Uh-uh."

Muff was about to leave for the evening. I decided to stay. It was Monday night. If Mom was truly gearing up for a Tuesday "departure," as she may have declared a few days before, it could happen at any time after midnight and I wanted to be at her side.

To create a softer ambience, Muff went to a nearby store to pick up a candle for us. Mom turned to me and asked me if I was tired.

"No, Mom, I'm here with you."

"You're a big boy now."

"Yes, Mom."

" . . . Are you ready to go to bed now?"

"Not yet, Mom. Muff's going to bring us a candle."

"How many?"

"One."

"Ten?"

"No, just one. That's all we need."

"Okay. . . . We had this day. I laughed so. It's the funniest experience to have a day in the house. . . .

Muff returned with an aromatherapy candle in a glass jar. Nina, an aide, came in to provide medication and take Mom to the bathroom. I walked Muff to the lobby. We hugged. I told her I would try to tee it up for Mom. She commented on my strength. I was not so sure.

I walked down the hall and took a seat on a padded bench outside Mom's room, waiting for Nina to finish. I shot a film in my mind's eye of the surreal, desolate hallway. I noticed a sad vase of plastic flowers on a table at one end. Piped-in music of the 1950s did little to enliven the place. I imagine it was intended to evoke nostalgia among the predominant resident demographic. Teresa Brewer—whom I enjoyed listening to as a kid—crooned "Till I Waltz Again With You"—some of its lyrics uncannily appropriate to the moment:

Though it may break your heart and mine
The minute when it's time to go
Remember, Dear, each word divine
That meant I love you so

Nina finished. I went in and kissed Mom goodnight.

"Are you ready to go to bed?" Mom inquired.

"No, Mom. I'm going to stay with you."

I sat there wondering if this would be my last conversation with her. Had I said all I needed to say? Had I asked her all I needed to ask? There was something that I had never discussed with her. I was curious, but it seemed so petty. But if I didn't ask then, I might never know. Then again, how reliable would an answer be at this point in her life? The debate went on in my head. Finally, I asked. "Daddy thought I should be an architect—what did you think?"

"I never thought being an architect was a very exciting thing."

I had derived great joy and a decent living from my architectural education and licensure, but ultimately found teaching to be more rewarding. I decided not to press the point. I was glad I asked, regardless of her response. I took it as a measure of validation of my experience in the profession.

I read the *Vidui* to Mom. "Lord, my God and God of the Universe, ..." Upon completing the confessional, I noticed the setting sun. "It's time for *Mincha Maariv* (afternoon and evening prayers). Do you want to pray?"

"No. If I can't sing to start, I can't sing to finish."

"It's up to you."

" . . . I love to hear that song."

"Which song, Mom?"

"Eight numbers in it."

I struggled to think of a song that had eight numbers in it. "Is it a song about Chanukah?"

"Probably."

On this night,
Let us light
One little candle fire.
'Tis a sight,
Oh so bright,
One little candle fire . . .

I lit the candle Muff had brought. I pulled the rolling dining table over and set the candle between us. We sat in relative stillness. A few birds still chattered outside as night had not fully arrived on the other side of our window curtains. Inside, there was a quiet hum—perhaps the refrigerator.

There was an occasional clearing of the throat and smacking of the lips from Mom. An occasional rumbling of my stomach—I had forgone an invitation to eat dinner. A single ring of the phone interrupted the silence. No one there. Then the air conditioner abruptly kicked on with a deep grumble that slowly swayed into a calm, steady resonance.

Mom, with only one eye visibly open in the dim light, moved her head back and forth, putting her finger to her mouth. Her eyes met mine. She ran her tongue around her lips and put her head back.

"I'm ready to go to sleep. My body is."

"How about the rest?"

"It's all ready. This light is just perfect."

A HEALING POEM FOR THE SON

Sitting in a room
with the frail shell
of what once was my
entire universe—
me outside in the light
struggling in darkness
as confining as the womb.
Does her heartbeat
linger in my unformed ears?
Does her warmth envelop me
in a sea of tears?
Does a food move between us
across the years?

Who or what lies in
the bed across this room?
No mortal matches
the memory of the Mother
who consumed me as I
consumed her.

Born of her loins,
cleaved from her,
ever moving toward separation—
a goal so harshly achieved.
Now in these final moments
can we reconnect, rekindle

a flame once so pervasive
now so dim?

I light a candle in
the sunset hour.
Its glow plays in our eyes
bringing soft music
to the night.
Harbinger of the final candle
like a shawl caressing
a forgotten hug.

We share the light—
a gentle glint
in graying eyes.

Our embrace—
a reunion, a reminder
of the gulf
that life and time
has rendered,
that death and time
increase,
that time and love
erase.

6

Sunday, September 16

TENSIONS ARE RUNNING HIGH. *Jeff and I have found ourselves unable to rationally discuss the funeral plans, or anything else. He becomes argumentative about what he perceives as my intention to delay the funeral for my convenience. He harangues me about Jewish law, and respect for the dead, and how it is a violation to delay a funeral.*

Mom's body will arrive Tuesday, the first day of Rosh Hashanah, so she can't be buried then. The same is likely true for Wednesday, given the cemetery's affiliation with a Conservative shul (synagogue) that observes a two-day holiday.

I offer two reasonable alternatives, neither of which seem acceptable to him. Friday would work best for me, allowing me to travel on Thursday, after the holiday. Alternatively, while it would not be my preference, if I were to travel on the second day of Rosh Hashanah, I can make a Thursday interment.

I can't make any sense out of him. Wednesday isn't really an option, but maybe that's what he is angling for. He complains that Thursday constitutes an unnecessary delay, and he's blaming me for it! He compounds that by stating that I should not absent myself from my community on the second day of Rosh Hashanah. I don't understand why that would be a concern of his. Maybe it's a dig about my affiliation with a Conservative congregation, given that we were raised in Reform Judaism where the holiday is typically a one-day event. He rejects Friday out of hand.

His crowning comment is calling me selfish for causing this fictitious delay. I'm being selfish for trying to make arrangements to be at my mother's funeral? His allegation is irrational, unfair, and hurtful. I am outraged and finally have to end the call. In addition to our scuttled plans, amity and sanity in the family is evaporating as well. I go into the next room and vent my feelings with Muff from whom I get a measure of sympathy.

SUNDAY EVENING'S MINYAN IS *much like Saturday's—no less potent. We are closer to forty people strong. Adam sets quite a tone with his heartfelt remembrance of his Granny. He makes us chuckle at the image of this* rebbetzin *casting for crabs at the Saint Simons Island pier. We well up with tears when Adam's own tears overcome him.*

Debbie follows with some humorous remarks about how she, at age twenty, met Mom at Jeff's ordination. At the party that evening, Mom—after a few drinks—said she'd "keep" Debbie. Debbie recounts all the things she learned from her mother-in-law, from cooking to crafts. She marvels at how Mom would buy huge quantities of pecans with each harvest and then meticulously cut each one to the perfect size for recipes requiring chopped nuts. She'd measure out one-cup portions and seal them in plastic bags to grab from the freezer whenever needed.

This evening, instead of reading again from my journal, I select favorite poems of others that capture my feelings. This one, by Jo Carson, reflects my gratitude at having had the conversations at her bedside throughout the summer.

I AM ASKING YOU TO COME BACK HOME

I am asking you to come back home
before you lose the chance of seein' me alive.
You already missed your daddy.
You missed your uncle Howard.
You missed Luciel.
I kept them and I buried them.
You showed up for the funerals.
Funerals are the easy part.
You even missed that dog you left.
I dug him a hole and put him in it.
It was a Sunday morning, but dead animals
don't wait no better than dead people.

My mamma used to say she could feel herself
runnin' short of breath of life. So can I.

And I am blessed tired of buryin' things I love.
Somebody else can do that job to me.
You'll be back here then; you come for funerals.

I'd rather you come back now and got my stories.
I've got whole lives of stories that belong to you.
I could fill you up with stories,
stories I ain't told nobody yet,
stories with your name, your blood in them.
Ain't nobody gonna hear them if you don't
and you ain't gonna hear them unless you get back home.

When I am dead, it will not matter
how hard you press your ear to the ground.

TOGETHER AND APART

There were intermittent connections and disconnections between my siblings and me throughout this saga. In June, we realized it was time for planning Mom's ultimate arrangements. From our disparate locations, Muff, Jeff, and I huddled together on the phone suggesting—more like debating—alternatives. Jeff proposed cremation as a cost-saving approach. Given his decades of officiating funerals, I figured he had worked with countless families who had chosen cremation. I didn't have that experience. I just knew that cremation is not a traditional Jewish option; it is explicitly prohibited among Orthodox and Conservative Jews, and discouraged if not prohibited among Reform. I was horrified that Jeff would make this a financial decision.

Additionally, whether it would be corpse or ashes, there was the selection of a final resting place to be determined. Dad was buried not far from Mom's parents at the Hebrew Benevolent Society Cemetery, a historic cemetery in Columbia. There was a plot designated for Mom adjacent to his. Since none of us lived near there, we considered options closer to each of us as well. The Hills of Eternity cemetery outside San Francisco had a number of our family's graves, so that seemed a reasonable alternative to me should we decide against Columbia.

It fell upon me to do some primary research. I was greatly relieved when I learned that the burial of ashes was not an option at the Hebrew Benevolent Society Cemetery. This obviated the need to debate the subject with Jeff. All I needed to do was provide a report of my findings, which I did:

I called Tree of Life Congregation in Columbia and got the name of Bernard Fleischman, 88 years old, who handles arrangements for Hebrew Benevolent Society Cemetery. He immediately recognized our lineage. In fact, he claimed to have dated Mom "before she got attracted to the rabbi!" He told me that since his first wife died, he has remarried an 82-year-old "chick." As Granny Hymson would say, he has a lot of piss and vinegar.

He told me that the spaces for Mom and Dad are provided gratis to clergy and spouse. He mentioned twice that a contribution to the Society would be in order nonetheless.

He said there were no ashes buried in HBS. He said they had refused to allow ashes to be interred in the past (even though there was no specific rule against it). His opinion was that it would be "out of line to have a cremation next to a rabbi"—that if we wanted cremation, there was "no place in the cemetery—check with any rabbi," he added. I didn't mention Jeff's profession, nor his opinion.

This corroborated the initial conversation I had had with the folks at the Dunbar funeral home.

I suppose we could do whatever we want anyway. However, this seems to be the cultural norm in this place. As for money, I have a detailed spreadsheet of all expenses which I will share if you like. If cremation is taken out of the picture, the dollars are very close in Riverside ($7,600), SFO ($8,800) and Columbia ($7,000 + donation which given the market price of plots in HBS Cemetery could reasonably be another $1,000).

It gets down to what we want to do and where we want to do it, rather than dollars. I am open to either Columbia or SFO. I see benefits and liabilities to each.

We'll tawk.
Bro

While such matters as final arrangements percolated, Muff and I continued to spend time with Mom. For various reasons, among them physical distance, Jeff was not always with us, including on Tuesday, August 7, when we thought Mom might die. Mom had asked about Jeff at one point. Truly, she—all of us, actually—missed our brother's presence that week. At the same time, we felt comfortable that all was for the best. Jeff was attending to what he needed to do, just as we were. He was at an annual retreat of southeastern clergy at Wildacres, a conference center in the Blue Ridge Mountains of North Carolina. This was an important part of his personal spiritual preparation for the imminent High Holy Days.

That Tuesday ended with little tangible evidence that it would be Mom's last day. As we often did, Muff and I exchanged glances and slowly left as Mom drifted off to sleep. We hugged in the hallway, and shared our fascination with all that had transpired.

As Muff departed, I went back to Mom's room. With the aid of a flash-light, I ate half of one of the sandwiches Muff had brought for our dinner. I wrote in my journal, worked another crossword puzzle, then sat in the still darkness for a while. As it grew later, and the "Tuesday" window was clos-ing, I found myself getting increasingly apprehensive. I nearly jumped out of my skin when at 10:45 p.m., Mom blasted sustained flatus punctuated by a guttural grunt. At eleven o'clock, I popped an Ambien with some ambiva-lence. I was not sure if taking a sedative constituted a breach of my duties as a sentry. As I walked back into the bedroom, a simple smacking of her lips sent a shudder up and down my spine. I was starting to concoct scenarios in my mind, and hoped that if I was to bear witness to her passing, it would go quietly and effortlessly. I wondered again about my sister's estimation of my "strength."

PART 2
Rachamim

רחמים
Compassion

There is no weed that would not rather be a flower.

—JEAN BALLON

COMPASSION

In Hebrew, the word for compassion is *rachamim*. The need for *rachmones*, the Yiddish equivalent, was something my father frequently spoke of. Both words are derived from *rechem*, Hebrew for womb. Where would compassion be more evident than in the love of a mother for the life growing inside her?

My experience in 2001 demonstrated that the path from separation to connection goes through compassion. Compassion may be variously defined as a genuine regard for others, a willingness to share in others' pleasures as well as their misfortunes, a desire that others experience joy and should be free from suffering, and/or the ability to bestow acceptance and forgiveness of the perceived imperfections of others. I should quickly add that self-compassion, the reflexive form of all the above behaviors, may be a prerequisite for compassion for others.

Throughout my family's story, whenever anyone demonstrated these qualities, compassion directly led to genuine connection. I see little distinction between an act of *compassion* and the sense of *connection*. Nonetheless, in this section, the focus is on the former.

Our story includes many blessedly compassionate acts. When Mom failed to find the environment she most greatly desired, leading to a sense of separation, the compassion of her children and other caregivers helped ease the situation. My siblings and I felt the pain of losing our mother, but we gained solace from our community and ultimately through our kinship. For me, the added alienation I suffered from the calamity of 9/11 was alleviated, to some degree, not so much by society suddenly seeing *my* pain amidst the immense national tragedy, but in the simple act of my *sharing* the pain of those most closely affected by the murderous attacks.

Disclaimer: few among us operate in a constant state of compassion. I suppose even the Dalai Lama has his off days. By citing instances where my compassion game was elevated, I by no means want to leave the false impression that I am headed for sainthood in this regard. The benefit in reflecting on those virtuous moments is that it encourages me to make a more concerted effort to exercise my compassion muscles in the future.

7

Monday, September 17

TODAY MARKS THE FINAL *day of* shiva—*not because we have fulfilled our obligation to mourn for seven days, but because at sunset, Rosh Hashanah begins. According to Jewish law,* shiva *must cease with the commencement of a holiday—even if the mourning period has begun only minutes before. The rabbi cannot be with us this morning, so he arranged for our prayers to be led by a fellow congregant who is very knowledgeable of the morning service.*

After hosting a houseful of people each of the preceding nights, we are just nine people this morning. Technically, we are short by one the requisite number in attendance for a minyan—*the quorum required for reciting the* Kaddish. *By me, we have sufficient "community" to recite the prayer. As my Granny Ballon would say, "Nit!" This literally translates as "not" in Yiddish, but in context I've always understood it to mean "No big deal!"*

Today is the last day of the Jewish month of Elul, and also the last day of the year 5761. Since boyhood, I have sounded the ram's horn in synagogue to mark the Jewish New Year. Throughout Elul, the month before Rosh Hashanah, the shofar is also sounded after morning prayers each day, in order to help us focus our attention and prepare ourselves spiritually for the solemn holidays to follow. As much of an honor as it has always been to sound shofar for the congregation on Rosh Hashanah, it is no less an honor to sound it in my own house to conclude our morning shiva *service. I take a deep breath, and let out a long clear blast with Mom foremost in my thoughts. Then, per custom, our family takes a ritual walk around the block, signifying our completion of* shiva *and our return to life outside the walls of our house.*

AFTER CONSULTATION WITH THE *rabbi, I have decided to fly to Columbia on the second day of Rosh Hashanah. Coming from a Reform background, where the holiday is typically celebrated for one day, I feel minimal discomfort. Furthermore, the rabbi has encouraged me to do whatever I have to do for Mom and the family. This will allow me to be in South Carolina for a funeral on Thursday.*

Among the family, I am the only one determined to attend. Muff thinks I'm crazy—that it's too dangerous to fly. My feeling is that people flew in blissful ignorance when security was lax, and now, when there is greater vigilance, everyone is staying home. That doesn't make much sense to me.

I receive no explanation as to why Jeff has decided not to be there. He has merely stated the fact that he will not be coming—all the more galling that he would bicker about the timing. It's a long but manageable drive, or a short flight, to get from his place in Punta Gorda, Florida to Columbia. I don't get it.

Fortunately, Jeff and I have both calmed down, and at least on the surface, we have been able to grant one another forgiveness before Rosh Hashanah as the Holy Days ask us to do. We make amends. For this I am extremely grateful—not only to Jeff, but to Judaism that gives us guidance and wisdom to seek and grant forgiveness.

It is a mixed blessing to have Rosh Hashanah so soon after Mom's death. On the one hand, it has preempted a full shiva *experience that I suspect would have been a greater source of comfort than this truncated version. On the other, Rosh Hashanah sets a useful context for reconciliation.*

As the revised plans are taking shape, the bat mitzvah last Saturday has me thinking—why can't we use the telephone to bring people to the funeral who otherwise would miss it? We teleconference all the time at the office. Why not a conference call at graveside? For all that I detest my cell phone, this is an opportunity for it to be of real service—especially its speaker-phone capability. We kick the idea around. Some think it's too weird. Some think it's weird enough to work. I call the office to find out how these things are set up. It's easy to do. I get a phone number from AT&T that anyone can call into on Thursday at 2:30 p.m. Eastern time. I email the information to the family. It will be a bit of a gamble. There is no assurance that my cell phone will even get a good signal at the cemetery—but what do we have to lose?

SELF-COMPASSION

If I want to develop *rachmones* for others, I must learn to accept and honor "differences" within myself, such as when I speak or act in ways that don't align with my higher values and aspirations. Accepting my own shortcomings is essential if I am to have the capacity to accept others. Developing self-compassion may be a challenge, but there's an opportunity to turn toward myself with the same tools that are available for improving relationships with others.

Listening is key. I have taken time to listen to myself. I listen to my subconscious—often by analyzing my dreams—and discover views held secretly within. This expands my understanding of who I am, and helps me move ahead with greater confidence and consideration. I am not unaware of my limitations. That's part of self-acceptance. There's a delicate balance between the divine discontent of striving for perfection, and the peace that comes from accepting something short of that ideal.

During my mother's decline, I was struck by a simple statement she made that reflected self-compassion and acceptance. It was on that first day of her expansive conversation, when her sweet reverence was on display. More than once, she let us know that she was quite content. This was very believable owing to the softness of her voice. "I'm happy. Perfectly."

Debbie asked her about her children. Mom's perplexing response: "My children are comfortable in their not knowing. My children have always known that they're unstable."

When we asked for some clarification, Mom added, "In my mind that's a good thing. . . . I think they're good. It's not perfect, but I don't think they expect it to be."

It was profound to hear her declare her happiness when she was enduring so many physical and mental challenges. I also knew something about the disappointments in her life, not the least of which was living nearly thirty years without the companionship of my father. Hers was a true expression of acceptance and peace.

8

Tuesday, September 18

Rosh Hashanah morning is *always a time of great meaning and joy for me. Sounding the ram's horn carries so much significance. It is a sound that makes people laugh or weep. It is strangely exciting, energizing, filled with nostalgia, even history. I first sounded the horn at my father's request forty years ago. He encouraged me to give everything I had to it, especially the final long blast—Tekiah Gedolah.*

For the past two years, Rosh Hashanah fell on a Saturday, and in the Conservative shul *that I attend, the shofar is not sounded on the Sabbath. To compensate for this, I wrote a guided meditation on the shofar. It was a stretch for some. Even so, the congregation sat quietly with their eyes closed as I led them in recalling and reflecting on the meaning of the ancient sounds.*

This year, the rabbi and I talked about what it would be like to bring that same consciousness to the actual sounds. So, I wrote a new guided meditation for the shofar service. Part of it led the congregants to imagine witnessing fire and brimstone at Sinai, and the walls tumbling at Jericho—both venues, according to scripture, of great and mighty blasts of the shofar. In the wake of current events, I knew such references could have horrible connotations if I left them as written. During the days that followed the attacks, I made some changes. I wanted to acknowledge the horrors we have all witnessed, while making a distinction between what is holy and what is evil.

Today, sitting in shul, *I feel more trepidation over the congregation's response to this untried meditation than I do over actually sounding the*

horn—which usually has my kishkes (guts) tied up in knots Rosh Hashanah morn. I anxiously go over the shofar service in my mind. When
I hear the Maftir (the last person called up to the Torah) begin chanting
the blessing after the Haftarah (reading from Prophets), I rise to my feet
and ascend the bimah. The shofar service is next. The rabbi prolongs my
agony by inserting a prayer for our congregation and then a prayer for
our country. At last, he graciously introduces the shofar service, letting
the congregation understand our motivation for creating the new guided
meditation.

Gently, I read to them . . . .

. . . Your journey moves on throughout the continuum of Jewish
history. All at once, you are at Sinai, you are at Jericho, you are
at every battle our people have fought. You are there, and you are
here in this sanctuary, still shaken by events of last week. Seven
days ago, you witnessed once again awesome fire, smoke, and
thunder descending from the sky. You witnessed walls tumbling
down with destructive might. Yet these terrifying sights were not
accompanied by the Divine sound of the shofar. These were offerings of evil, of man at his worst. If God's presence was observed at
all in New York, in Washington, and in the skies above Pennsylvania, it was not by might nor by power, but through the spirit of
brave and selfless individuals. God's presence has been observed in
the acts of love and kindness that have poured forth from people
the world over . . .

I feel my spine shiver when I get to the words about the attacks.
When I feel something like that, I tend to believe that others may share
in the emotion.

I chant the blessings and sound the shofar. It goes fine. More reading.
More shofar blasts. More reading. More blasts, and then the final loudest,
longest blast—Tekiah Gedolah. I fill my lungs. I close my eyes. I let the
sound pour through me in blackness, holding close to me thoughts of both
of my parents, letting them give me strength. It is breathtaking for me in
every sense of the word.

ATONEMENT

Our misdeeds separate us from one another. Our attempts at atonement
are designed to repair rifts. Virtually every Jew is at least aware of an annual obligation to confess and atone for misdeeds on the Day of Atonement
each fall. There are other opportunities, if not obligations, for confession of

which I imagine most liberal Jews are unaware. At least for me, it came to my awareness relatively late in life that in addition to the Yom Kippur and the deathbed confessionals, the liturgy includes a nightly bedtime *vidui* as well.

ON THE TUESDAY THAT we thought might be Mom's last day on earth, I woke up on the floor of her room relieved that she was still very much alive. When the aide came, I left for a long walk through the neighboring golf course. Upon my return, Mom was dressed, lying in bed. She gave me a typical southern greeting, "Hey." Her first question of the day was, "Is that my stone wall?"

I did not see the wall, so I said it was. I asked what was on the other side. She did not know. I took the remote out of her hand and turned off the muted TV that only the aide would have turned on. Mom closed her eyes and mumbled something about the stone wall. We remained silent as she drifted off.

I had been sitting in the wheelchair placed beside the bed. I rose from it and it creaked, causing her to waken. I swapped out the wheelchair for one of her wicker club chairs, lest that happen again. We sat speechless, looking at one another. Finally, I said I would meditate. Adjusting the chair to face her, with my arms supported by a semicircle of brittle woven straw, I closed my eyes and silently recited a mantra of *shalom*, drawing peace from above as I inhaled, sending peace to her as I exhaled. When I opened my eyes, Mom was back to sleep, her midsection occasionally rising and falling with an irregular rhythm.

Earlier, during my walk, I had prayed to be a healer and poet that day. Those words had spontaneously arisen in my prayer and surprised me when they did. When I thought about them, the message came that my healing must be self-directed. As I had often done in the past, I must use my poetry for my own healing. Like oxygen masks on an airplane, through self-healing I would be better able to bring healing to Mom—not the other way around. I wrote "A Healing Poem for the Son."

WE WERE STILL A month and a half away from the Jewish New Year, the season of reflection, for acknowledging our misdeeds and seeking atonement. So it was startling when Mom, *mittendrinnen* (out of the blue), uttered the traditional greeting for Rosh Hashanah, "*L'shana tova* (For a good year)." She went on, "I don't know if I approve of that."

"Approve of what?" I responded.

"*L'shana tova.*"

"Why?"

"I don't know if it's such a great date."

That was eerily prophetic. Was she so clear about the Jewish calendar and her internal clock that she realized she would not make it to the High Holy Days?

"Look at that . . . Douglas . . . your spirit!" She seemed to see it hovering above me and to the right, over the bed. "Are there a lot more people than us that believe in spirits?"

"What?"

"You look like you have the answer," she declared.

I was completely baffled. "I don't even know the question. You have as many answers as I have."

Huh? Mom believed in spirits!!!

It was a day of conversation—some understandable, some not. As the evening wore on, Muff and I could see that Mom was clearly not ready for sleep as she continued to engage us in conversation.

I gave Mom a hug and some kisses. She asked why. I said I thought she had liked it the previous night. She said she did, that it was special, and that each one got to be more special. I offered that Muff and I would each kiss her goodnight and then we'd be quiet for fifteen minutes as she used to do with us as children. Mom replied, "She should be here—the person who is involved in this event." I suggested to Mom that she should invite that person into the room to ask for her help—and reminded Mom that on Saturday, she herself had talked about making the unthinkable thinkable by asking for help. Mom replied that she would think about it, and that Jeff should know. I told her that I would write it down. I took some notes, then proposed that Mom close her eyes—that I would close mine, too, and we would try being quiet for fifteen minutes. I took a deep breath and closed my eyes. I didn't even look to see Mom or Muff's response. I just began meditating on *shalom*. Then, other words of invocation came to mind and I recited them silently. Suddenly, it occurred to me that the "She" mom was referring to might be the *Shekhinah*, the feminine Divine spirit. Even if that was not her meaning, why not call in the *Shekhinah* to bring peaceful energy to Mom. So, I did.

I meditated *shalom* some more, and then, slowly, brought my awareness back to the room and opened my eyes. Mom was resting peacefully.

9

Wednesday, September 19

TODAY, I SET OUT *on my journey to South Carolina and my mother's funeral—a unique event in anyone's life. United Airlines told me to arrive at San Jose International Airport three hours before my 6:25 a.m. departure. They didn't bother to mention that no one would be behind their darkened counter at that hour, or that the gates would be entirely inaccessible until 5:00 a.m.*

When I arrive at 4:00 a.m., I become the ninth person in line. I pick up my journal and sit on my carry-on bag, a sea of black and white terrazzo surrounding me. My focus is on the page, but I sense the line of other hopeful travelers slowly lengthening behind me. At first, I am the only one to push my luggage on its side and sit on it. A few more try it. Why everyone else is content to stand for hours on this hard floor is beyond me.

It is too bright in here for this time of the morning—and too creepy. Canned guitar music plays over the public address system, interrupted periodically by a recorded announcement welcoming people to the airport and reciting the latest security rules.

A few minutes before 5:00—there are signs of life behind the counter. The lights go on. It looks like one agent has started working. The line ahead of me tightens up. I get to my feet—whoa! Where did all these people come from? Surrounded by legs, my vision was obscured, and I didn't realize how many travelers had entered the terminal in the last hour. There are scores of people at all the airline counters now. The line behind me is a hundred feet long.

I have my boarding pass by 5:06, and I quickly appreciate having arrived at 4:00. I head for the gate and observe the stunned look on the face of a woman asking, "Is this the United line?" The security checkpoint has increased its rigor in the wake of the attacks—more inspectors, more scrutiny, more police. I haven't had anyone look so closely at my I.D. since I traveled in the Soviet Union.

Beyond the checkpoint, I find myself looking at faces a little differently. As a man in pilot's garb passes me on his way to his gate, I wonder, "Is this the face of a hero? Will he be in a life-or-death struggle in the skies?" Sitting at my gate, I shamefully engage in racial profiling by taking a second look at two well-groomed businessmen chatting it up, who happen to have a Middle Eastern appearance. Then, for very different reasons, I find myself noticing gray-haired women traveling alone.

The plane touches down at O'Hare International Airport, ending the first leg of my journey. The captain welcomes us to Chicago in the customary manner, then adds the words, "God bless America." An uneventful flight—the kind we all prayed for. I dash a great distance in a short time to get to the departure gate for the Columbia leg. I've always admired architect Helmut Jahn's United Airlines Terminal—derivative and reminiscent of the great train stations of Europe. Today, large American flags hang in its steel-webbed atrium.

MY ARRIVAL AT THE *Columbia airport is perhaps the most significant indication of the fallout from the attacks. In years past, I would have been greeted by Linda's smiling face at the gate. Today, not only is my cousin absent, so is everyone else. The airport is abandoned. I walk past empty shop after empty shop, all the way to the curb. When I get there, it is ominously guarded by police, and the parking spaces are blocked by orange cones. Two or three people stand about waiting for rides. Linda is nowhere in sight. My passing concerns are allayed when she finally arrives. She has been delayed, waiting in a line of cars to have her vehicle inspected for bombs or other contraband.*

Soon, we get back to Linda's red brick house in a gated community adjacent to the Fort Jackson army base. I have just about enough time to wash up and change my clothes before leaving for minyan. *On Monday, I had called Temple Beth Shalom, the Conservative congregation, and was told that they would be conducting a* minyan *at 6:00 p.m. today. Linda gives me directions and the keys to her car. After a pleasant ride, I arrive at the suburban* shul *about fifteen minutes early. There is not a single car in the parking lot, and over the course of the next twenty minutes, none arrive. Clearly the office had given me false information. There is no evening* minyan *this second day of Rosh Hashanah. It had been my intention to recite* Kaddish *for Mom. I decide, under the circumstances, that my good intentions would have to suffice.*

Linda had mentioned to me that the Reform congregation is also on Trenholm Road. I had already been told that they would not be having a minyan. *Nevertheless, I decide to go there just for old time's sake. This had been my father's first pulpit. When I arrive at Tree of Life Congregation, there is a small queue of cars with parents awaiting their children's dismissal from religious school. I enter through the school wing and find my way to the administrative office. I ask a woman if the rabbi is available. She asks me the nature of my business. The words catch in my throat as I mention that he will be officiating my mother's funeral tomorrow. She instantly becomes sympathetic, and says the rabbi will be available shortly. At my request, she shows me to the sanctuary where I sit in meditation until his arrival.*

The rabbi greets me and immediately comments on my physical resemblance to Jeff.

This unanticipated meeting is very useful, and would not have occurred had there been a minyan *at Temple Beth Shalom. We are able to confer on the logistics of the funeral and* shiva. *He gives me a referral for handling Mom's stone marker. Probably most important is that I will not be meeting a total stranger at graveside tomorrow.*

As we leave the sanctuary, I ask how long it has been in its present configuration. It seems different from my recollection—a memory that was formed nearly twenty-seven years earlier at the funeral service for my father. I then learn that this is an altogether different site and structure, the congregation having moved out from their original downtown location fifteen years ago.

I return to Linda's. She and Mike have prepared dinner. Between Kyle and Hunter, their irrepressible grade-school boys, their two terriers, and the neighbor's retriever, it is a lively meal. After dinner, Linda and I talk until our eyelids droop.

I go upstairs to their comfortable guest suite and open my journal briefly. Despite being three time zones removed, I am eager to go to sleep.

A PRETTY NOSE

I was about to bury my Mom, but not all the mixed thoughts and feelings I had about her. I could not reflect on her life and our relationship without acknowledging its challenges. Not that I spoke of them at the funeral, but in these days, I feel it is necessary to examine the whole picture. To do otherwise would deny me the opportunity to render upon our relationship the compassion it deserves. We each had our issues. When they collided, it could be most unpleasant. Some forgiveness and acceptance is in order.

Mom did not want to be eulogized—she made that perfectly clear. Nor, I suppose, would she wish to be castigated. One of the wonderful aspects of Judaism is that we don't idealize our heroes. We present them, warts and all. Recognizing their flaws makes them more relatable, and leaves room for acceptance of our own flaws. Let this chronicle be no exception.

To make a recitation of my mother's shortcomings might be considered unkind if it weren't provided in a larger context. Where the Torah provides its greatest inspiration is in recounting the evolution of its imperfect heroes and how they overcame some of their prior failings. Jacob, who famously swindled his brother Esau out of his birthright, later wrestled with God, after which he was renamed Israel, which literally means "God wrestler." His spiritual transformation became the eponym for our people. We are the Children of Israel—not of Abraham or Moses. As such, we have inherited the capacity to grapple with both the Divine and our own limitations—as surely Mom did. Moreover, Maimonides, the great medieval Sephardic Jewish philosopher, taught that those who atone for a misdeed and change their ways are held closer to God than those who have never sinned.

MOM USED TO SAY that if she had had a pretty nose, she would have been absolutely impossible to live with because she already had a pretty high opinion of her many other fine qualities. It was a big nose that gave her some humility—well, sort of.

She was a blustery, cocky, loud, brash, spontaneous, hard-driving, often irritating, often arrogant woman—all this, along with her warmth, charm, uproarious sense of humor, inquisitive mind, sense of adventure, fierce determination, diligence, community spirit, diverse creative talents, and fundamentally loving soul.

She was a woman of contradictions.

She had an ability to truly empathize, to connect with somebody deeply and intuitively, and, consequently, to say or do exactly what that person most needed. They may not have even been aware of their needs themselves.

The flip side of that trait was that when she was pissed, that same intuition allowed her to say or do exactly what most hurt. It could be as simple as a piercing glance to warn us that we had crossed some inviolable line. At other times, it was physical. She was adept at inflicting the occasional subtle-but-effective pinch on the arm. That got our attention. There also were uncommon moments of such outrage that she, as would Dad, applied belt to *tush*. Such corporal punishment sounds horribly abusive through a twenty-first-century lens, but it seemed normal back then.

Mom appreciated the characterization of native Israelis as *Sabras*, the name originally given to Israel's indigenous prickly pears that are tough on the outside, but delicate and sweet on the inside. No doubt she could identify with that. On the other hand, she also had no problem turning on the southern charm on the outside while masking different feelings within. After all, one of her favorite sayings was, "Be sincere, even if you don't mean it!"

I CAN ONLY ASSESS Mom's parenting skills from my perspective as the "baby" of the family—a status that Mom, to my chagrin, worked overtime to maintain. She did things for me when I should have been developing a greater sense of independence—more or less well-meaning indulgences that had deleterious effects. Sometimes they caused me embarrassment, such as the time that my classmates laughed at me in disbelief when I asked our second-grade teacher if she would tie my shoe. I didn't know that all the others had already developed this skill, since Mom was still doing this for her little boy.

Of greater consequence—although I didn't recognize it at the time—was that when an elementary school report was due, she'd be in there with the encyclopedia and the typewriter transcribing large sections of information about whatever topic I was supposedly reporting on. I would select the passages to plagiarize and create the eye-catching cover art, but mostly bypassed the essential skill of doing genuine research in a timely manner. It was an unfortunate symbiosis. I got my needs met in a blissfully indolent way while she fulfilled her desire to protect me from the pain of growing up. It took me years to develop the study skills and independent thinking necessary to meet my academic responsibilities, as well as to develop a real thirst for knowledge.

She meant well.

Mom was not like other mothers, if only because, like our whole family, she was in the public eye. I suppose we all had a love/hate relationship with that role. Mom was fine being the *rebbetzin* as long as it was on *her* terms. She redefined the role so narrowly that no one before or since would fit it as uniquely as she. When she wanted to act as a leader among the women, she did. When she wanted to say, "Go f- 'em!"—without hesitation she did that, too, quite explicitly. Our dear friend Julia Mirel, wife of my buddy from childhood, Rabbi Jim Mirel, quoted Mom's pithy advice to a new *rebbetzin*:

> The ones who love you will love you, no matter what you do. The
> ones who don't like you won't like you, no matter what you do.
> So, do what you damn please!

My mother, for all of her many fine attributes, had—as all of us do—a shadow side. I didn't give it a second thought as a kid, but reflecting back, this was a woman who pretty much needed a daily shot of Scotch or vodka and some Empirin Compound tablets to get through the dinner hour. Whether that constituted any kind of substance abuse or addiction, I can't really say, but something inside her clearly was in pain and needed to be soothed.

From many conversations with her over the years, I know that Mom consciously suffered from a self-declared inferiority complex. Maybe it stemmed from her childhood and how her older brothers taunted and teased her unmercifully. In my own struggle with low self-esteem, I've learned that the ego can operate in several ways. A healthy approach is to live with a level of confidence balanced with a dose of humility. The shadow version of that, as it was with Mom, is to suffer feelings of worthlessness masked by arrogance.

Some say, "If you spot it, you got it!" In that regard, I am very familiar with many of Mom's foibles. They have been my frequent companions and may never fully depart, even as I make incremental progress toward overcoming them.

Ultimately, I think of one of Granny Hymson's frequent maxims: "You've got to take the bitter with the better." I'm willing to do that with Mom. Acceptance and forgiveness are much easier to live with than resentment. Of course, there was the time in second grade when I wanted a plain brown briefcase like the one my friend Charlie Gordon had. Mom, I'm sure out of her great love for me and her exuberant quest to decorate the world, got me a black briefcase emblazoned with an image of Hopalong Cassidy astride his trusty white stallion, Topper. But I'm over that now, right?

Clearly, I shared Mom's love of art, but our aesthetic tastes became increasingly divergent. After Dad's death, I was unhappy with Mom's choice of the headstone spanning their two plots. It continued to irk me when I returned to Columbia for Mom's funeral. I'm long overdue in letting go of that judgement. It's past time for me to acknowledge Mom's right to her own aesthetic opinions, to recognize that she made an effort to select something that was tasteful, elegant, simple, and quiet in a way—while still uniquely calling attention to itself in another way—a true reflection of her values. Even though our aesthetic sensibilities differed, I owe my underlying artistic passion to Mom. We shared a burning desire to create, to beautify, and to delight the visual senses. It's so much less anxiety-provoking to simply let go of our differences and bask in appreciation and compassion.

POLARITY

They say that opposites attract, and no doubt that was much of the appeal between Mom and Dad. I've also heard it said that those same divergent styles, over time, can become increasingly irritating. No doubt my parents experienced both the fire and the ice of their divergent personalities. Nonetheless, they were pretty good at keeping any such friction to themselves. I suspect that was out of compassion as much for the family as for one another. It was all in the spirit of *shalom bayit*—the Jewish value of maintaining a peaceful home environment.

Dad was a Yankee, born in Pawtucket, Rhode Island to very traditional and Jewishly observant immigrants from Odessa. He was raised in neighboring Providence, where he won math and Latin prizes at the prestigious Classical High School. He went on to graduate *magna cum laude* from Brown University, where he also distinguished himself as a member of the Phi Beta Kappa academic honor society. He received his rabbinical ordination from Hebrew Union College. Most of his life was devoted to serving his congregation seemingly seven days a week, often well into the evening. He was a quiet, reserved, respectful, reverent man. He rooted for the New York Giants baseball team, back in the day.

Mom was his polar opposite in many ways—a southerner through and through, born in Savannah, Georgia, the product of a relatively assimilated Jewish family. While some of her clan were born in the old country—Lithuania or Poland, depending on where the border was drawn at the time—her mom was born in New York City. Mom had no formal education after high school. Her lack of college may have had more to do with family economics and/or sexism than a lack of academic ability. Rather than a career, she focused on volunteering on behalf of the temple and other Jewish and community organizations, as well as on sustaining her home and family. She wore the title *rebbetzin* proudly, even as she defied any preconceptions, definitions, or expectations others might have had for the role. She had engaging wit and devil-may-care flair, and seemed more inclined to flaunt irreverence than demonstrate piety. Also, having grown up in Louisville down the block from future Hall-of-Famer Brooklyn Dodger shortstop Pee Wee Reese, Mom was an ardent Dodger fan.

Opposites may attract, but a marriage is sustained by important areas of congruence, creating opportunities to synergize by taking advantage of complementary skills and perspectives. While they were raised in very different Jewish environments, my parents found common ground in Reform Judaism. When Dad arrived at his first pulpit, Mom was already an active member. Her continued involvement in temple life, individualistic as it may have been, was nonetheless sincere. My parents created a "Jewish home," with Mom, no doubt, taking the lead. We had ritual objects and Jewish and Israeli art on display, and we celebrated Shabbat and holiday dinners with full gusto—all the symbolic essentials of a Jewish home.

Some differences in their Jewish upbringing were a potential source of tension, especially in the kitchen. Jewish dietary laws had not been observed in Mom's more secular home. It must have been a challenge, and a true indicator of her love for Dad, for her to meet my father's desire . . . not for a kosher home exactly, but for disallowing blatant *treif* (non-kosher food) such as pork and shellfish. Perhaps that was a compromise between two more extreme positions. It was never explained to us how that evolved.

Mom loved to tell the story about the first rabbinical conference she attended with Dad. As they sat at a dinner table with several other rabbis and their wives, the waiter asked for Mom's order. She passed up the tempting lobster in deference to Dad and his colleagues, only to be dismayed to hear just about everyone else—rabbis included—go for the *treif!* She never made that mistake again.

Dad had a pretty good idea of Mom's culinary preferences, and a high degree of tolerance. Joe Loewy, a friend and fellow congregant, shared the story of a time he was on a road trip with his parents and mine. Janet, his mom, had brought roast beef, corned beef, and ham sandwiches along for the car ride. Mom grabbed the first ham sandwich and playfully exclaimed, "Janet, this is a terrific roast beef sandwich!" Joe then caught a glimpse of Dad with a "twinkle in his eye and Mona Lisa smile." A generation later, when my niece, Jeff's daughter Sara, asked her Granny a question about *kashrut* (dietary laws), Mom summarized her thoughts on the subject: "It's more important what comes out of your mouth than what goes into it."

Jean and Sidney, Western Wall, Jerusalem, c. 1966

10

Thursday, September 20

MY NIGHT IS NOT *without incident. In the early morning hours before sunrise, I have a "lucid dream." Lucid dreams are a phenomenon in which the dreamer remains asleep and in dream state, while simultaneously having a conscious awareness that he or she is dreaming. These rare, mysterious experiences possess great power. I sense them like an electric charge throughout my entire nervous system. I don't know what spiritual significance my New Age friends ascribe to lucid dreams, but for me to have this experience on the eve of my mother's funeral indeed seems significant. The power of this dream is memorable—sadly, the content, like most dreams, quickly forgotten.*

The rest of this morning is all business. Linda and I traipse all over Columbia in preparation for the funeral. After a bite at Manhattan Bagels, we head for the Hebrew Benevolent Society Cemetery—a patch of ground adjacent to downtown Columbia, dating back to 1826. It is a small, humble cemetery, beautifully maintained. We walk right to the Ballon marker that Mom had placed at the head of their side-by-side graves after Dad's death.

I never liked this marker. It is white marble, post-lintel construction, about three and a half feet wide, rising about two and a half feet above the ground. The rectilinear pieces are some eight inches on edge. The faces are entirely without adornment other than the family name in all caps on the front and back of the cross piece.

I object to it for several reasons. First of all, Jewish monuments are supposed to be solid, without holes to speak of, although one could argue whether the space under the lintel technically constitutes a hole. Secondly, it just doesn't seem to fit with the other monuments in the cemetery. Even after nearly thirty years, its stone is whiter and brighter, and the shape is like none other. Thirdly, Mom decided to attach a marble vase to the center of the base, directly beneath the name BALLON. That makes no sense to me. It is Jewish tradition to place stones—not flowers—at a gravesite upon visitation. So, the empty vase just sits there. Finally, and what admittedly irked me most from the beginning, Mom asked for my input on the design of the stone and then, characteristically, went off and did her own thing anyway.

From the looks of things, I suspect the grave excavation had been prepared last week. It is boarded over. Tarps and some of the standard cemetery fake-grass carpeting are covering the pile of dirt next to it. I would have preferred for them to have piled the dirt somewhere other than on top of Dad's grave, but from a practical point of view, I suppose that was easiest since Mom's grave has a landscaped bed on the other side. I pull the coverings up to reveal Dad's footstone. The light of day sends scores of ants scurrying. I place a small stone on Dad's marker. I take some photographs so my siblings and I will be able to discuss what we will want to do for Mom. Then, Linda and I walk about the tiny cemetery checking in on other family and friends, most notably Charlie and Ida Hymson, our mutual grandparents.

Ballon grave marker, Hebrew Benevolent Society Cemetery,
Columbia, South Carolina

The next stop is Brun's Monuments on Two Notch Road. We walk in and I start to introduce myself. No sooner do I mention my name than the proprietor interrupts me, finishing my sentence by saying that I want to see about a grave marker for my mother. He has done his homework, or the rabbi has tipped him off, or both. Anyway, he takes a lot of the guesswork out of my task. He knows exactly what he had provided for Dad. We quickly conduct business, with the only outstanding issue being what the exact inscription will be.

There's nothing like a family business in a small town. Columbia may not be the smallest of towns, but it does feel that way at times. The stone carver is proud—not only because he has carved stone since he was twelve years old, or because he has been a master stone carver since age sixteen, but because he has such a strong personal involvement with and memory of just about every customer he has served all these years.

At our next stop, the folks of Greenlawn Mortuary are the way folks in mortuaries tend to be—somewhere between sympathetic and synthetic. I am pleased, however, despite my giving them no notice, that they give me an opportunity to view Mom. At first, the funeral director resists. "This is not planned as an open-casket affair," he tells me. I'm too unaware to interpret that as meaning they have not provided the requisite cosmetic services to make Mom presentable for viewing. I explain that I want to take a quick look to confirm for my sake and others that Mom has indeed arrived. He assures me that all the papers are in order and that I have nothing to worry about. He also contends that he is about to leave for another family's funeral. I assure him I will be brief. He relents.

I'm not entirely sure why it is so important for me to see her. It is just something I need to do—perhaps to take her death out of the realm of abstraction. I anguished about the possibility of confronting Mom's death those nights I stayed with her. As it turned out, she died alone. An aide discovered her, and Muff and Alan stayed with her remains until the mortuary in Riverside whisked her away. If I was coming this distance to bury her, I damn well ought to get the full visceral experience.

Some scurrying must be going on behind the scenes to get Mom all dolled up for me. I walk into the viewing room. I know that Muff and Alan went to Casket Warehouse—the Costco of caskets—and purchased a plain pine casket. That's the traditional Jewish practice—to reflect that in death we are all equal. I'd forgotten what that looks like. Dad's coffin had a coat of stain. This one is bare, unfinished wood. I vaguely notice the Star of David affixed to the top. As I recall, Mom objected to that symbol when it was proposed for Dad's casket decades before. "Too Jewish," she exclaimed. Nonetheless, I don't ask them to remove it.

The funeral director opens the upper part of the lid. It is Mom. I stare at her drawn, powdered face for a few seconds at most. With this gentleman pressed for time at my side, it seems much longer. Inexplicably and ridiculously, she reminds me of the actress Sissy Spacek. I am un-moved by the experience. In some ways, Mom looked more dead to me in her final days in Riverside. This proposed confrontation with reality is actually more of an abstraction. Nothing happens. Kissing her, saying goodbye to her, praying for her all seem like possibilities. I do none of that. I merely thank him, tell him I am done, and we leave.

The rest of the morning consists of working with Linda in prepara-tion for an unknown number of houseguests for a shiva *service after the funeral. We shop. We prepare trays—cold cuts and other assorted snacks.*

By one o'clock or so, I need some time and space to myself. I need to stop the busy-ness and prepare myself for the funeral. I go to my room and meditate. Somehow, from somewhere, as often happens, words come to me—words that I know I will share at the funeral. I am extremely grateful for the gift of words. I rarely take time to acknowledge this bless-ing, yet I would feel greatly diminished without it. With two logophile parents, I come by it honestly.

At last, it's time to leave for the cemetery. Mike drives. Linda insists that I sit up front, next to him. As we drive along, I reflect on the morning that Muff drove Jacob and me to Mom's at the end of my six-day visit in August. I wondered, then, if it would be my last visit with Mom. This time I know it is to be farewell. A few tears come, much as they had that day, though this time I quickly stifle them.

At graveside, a few local friends and family start to assemble. The tarps and Astro-Turf have been fully restored and are again covering Dad's stone. A spray of flowers is lying on the bare pine box. The rabbi drives up wearing a wide-brimmed black hat that, I'm glad to say, he leaves in his car in favor of a black kippah *(skullcap). After greeting a few people, my attention goes to initiating the conference call.*

I carefully punch in the number and password. I am the first one on the line. It is exactly 2:30. Quickly, I hear a beep as Daniel comes on the call, followed shortly by Ann Lois. Then participants join in a flurry, speaking over one another so I don't get all their names. In all, we have close to twenty callers from California, Texas, Florida, New York, and Costa Rica.

It's time to begin. The concept of having so many people attending a funeral via conference call lends a certain absurdity to the proceed-ings. This leads me to suggest to all that we make an effort to conduct the ceremony with the usual dignity one would expect at a funeral. For the most part, dignity prevails. One unanticipated problem, however, is the frequent commentary by Anita, Uncle Junie's second wife, sadly suffering from Alzheimer's Disease. Her random comments are a distraction. Junie, who had clearly expressed his love for Mom in his letter weeks ago, is devoted to Anita's care. If it means that we have to endure a fraction of the challenge he faces on a daily basis in order for him to be a part of the funeral, so be it.

The rabbi chants some Hebrew and recites some English prayers. He turns to me for a few remarks. For as long as I can remember, Mom was adamant about not being eulogized. "If they didn't know me when I was alive, they don't need to hear about me when I'm dead." With that in mind, I confine my remarks to some excerpts from my journal, concluding with the Pirke Avot *selection and the words I had scribed only an hour before:*

> *When we die it is neither silver nor gold nor gems nor pearls that accompany us, but Torah and good deeds only.*
> —Pirke Avot

> *How much Torah*
> *she knew?*
> *Probably more than*
> *she let on.*
> *In her final days—*
> *Yiddishkeit*
> *Judaism*
> *Hebrew*
> *God*
> *Pirke Avot—*
> *her thoughts turned to Torah.*
> *And in all her years—*
> *cooking*
> *sewing*
> *arts and crafts*
> *theater*
> *temple*
> *sisterhood—*
> *her good deeds were beyond measure.*
> *No eulogy*
> *she demanded,*
> *and no eulogy*
> *she receives—*
> *None at least that can*

summarize her unique presence.
Suffice it to say
as she leaves
this world
she goes not
unaccompanied.

The rabbi follows up mostly by quoting an email Jeff had sent to his southern rabbinical colleagues with whom he had been on retreat at the time I was visiting Mom in early August. Those days were rich for Jeff. He had been with Mom earlier in the summer and came to see her again on Labor Day, but it was difficult for him not to be with us that week. While he was on retreat, I told him the Pirke Avot *story. The next day, Jeff led his gathering of rabbis in worship. Included in the service that morning was a tribute to the memory of a vibrant woman in their community who had recently died. This prompted Jeff to share his experience navigating the impending death of his mother, thousands of miles away. He related the* Pirke Avot *story with them, as well. It was profound for all of them, and the subsequent tribute to their departed colleague was all the more deeply felt.*

At graveside, the rabbi concludes his remarks. He chants, in Hebrew, the traditional graveside prayer, El Maleh Rachamim, *followed by an English translation:*

> *O God full of compassion, Eternal Spirit of the universe, grant perfect rest under the wings of Your Presence to the soul of Jean Ballon, who has entered eternity. Master of Mercy, let her find refuge forever in the shadow of your wings, and let her soul be held up in the bond of eternal life. The Eternal God is her inheritance. May she rest in peace, and let us say: Amen.*

Slowly, the casket starts being lowered into the earth. The funeral director seizes the flowers that are lying on the casket and hands them to me. Quickly, I unwrap them. I look at the empty marble vase beneath the post and lintel marker. I look down at the long-stemmed bouquet in my hands, snap the stems in half, and stuff them into the vase, which, at least on this day, is fulfilling its purpose.

As the casket descends, Bernie Fleischman comes over to talk to me about his memories of Mom and Dad. He's the man who, back in June, gave me information about the cemetery rules, and mentioned that he had dated Mom before Dad came to town. He probably is unaware that his sonorous drawl is picked up by the speakerphone for the enjoyment of all our remote guests, who would otherwise have been listening to—pardon the expression—dead air.

With the casket fully lowered, the rabbi instructs us to follow the tradition of throwing earth on it. For some reason, a shovel is nowhere to be found. That makes little difference to me. Twenty-seven years earlier, at Dad's funeral, I had intentionally eschewed the shovel in favor of my hands. The red South Carolina clay stuck beneath my fingernails that day, as a tangible reminder of my father and the last mitzvah *I would perform for him. They say that burying the dead is the greatest* mitzvah *because it is a deed one performs with absolutely no chance or hope of having that person return the favor.*

Even if there were a shovel at Mom's interment, I had no intention of using it. I tug at the coverings, exposing the mound of earth and, once again, Dad's footstone. Again, ants scramble. I sink both hands with widespread fingers into the moist soil, bring them together like a small steam shovel, and lift my cargo over the void above my mother's casket. Opening my hands, I watch the clayey soil fall with a hollow clatter below, rendering a dark red blemish on the pristine pine. I step aside, allowing others to follow suit, and return to my post next to the rabbi. I examine the red bits beneath my nails.

When the scattering of earth is complete, the rabbi reads a psalm. Then we all recite Kaddish. *While the technology does not allow us to hear everyone on the conference call at once, fragments of different voices cut in and out, bringing us all together as a family.*

The rites are complete. I then ask if our virtual guests have anything to add. Jeff asks for me to state who is in attendance at graveside. I pass the cell phone around so all can introduce themselves and add whatever thoughts they so desire. Debbie asks me to give a description of the scene. I oblige, telling them about the quaint old cemetery—its brick walls, the stones, the open grave, the rows of chairs under a protective canopy providing potential shelter from impending rain. Then people say goodbye as one by one they sign off.

Hearing their goodbyes brings a tear to my eye. It is the only one I shed at graveside. I had been anticipating a great emotional release here. I suppose that facilitating the conference call may have forced me to be a bit too composed to cry at my mother's funeral. After the final goodbye, I close the lid of my flip phone, ending the call. I turn my attention to those present, receiving hugs and words of condolence from all. Soon, we pile into the cars to return to Linda's.

Hebrew Benevolent Society Cemetery, Columbia, South Carolina

Judging from the feedback I get later, in some ways the funeral had greater emotional impact on those who dialed in than those on site. I can only imagine that there was a tension at not being present, plus vivid mental image-making, like listening to old-time radio, that made the experience very tangible to the callers—virtual reality outperforming reality itself.

Shiva at Linda's is fine. Food. Conversation. Family and friends. Only later in the afternoon do I discover that it is Linda's birthday. In her selfless way, she hasn't said a word.

The evening wears on and becomes tiresome—the sound of the South Carolina football game in the living room, the banter, the echoes of a long day and a long journey. Again, Linda and I shut the place down.

I am enjoying the quiet solitude of the guest room. I prepare my things for travel home in the morning. It's time to read some, then turn out the light.

TEARS

My lack of tears at graveside surprised me a bit, given all the tears that arose anticipating this day. Generally, my tears come unanticipated, such as late one night in June, when Debbie and I were driving back from our visit with Mom. We were still on the road to Palo Alto, a good hour from home, when the cell phone rang. Muff reported that Mom had been taken to the ER again—this time with a prolonged seizure. I didn't want to admit that I was beginning to hope for a speedy end to her struggles. Debbie offered to take the wheel as tears began to run down my cheeks. My tears oddly raised a distant memory of the night when my Mom and Dad had returned to our home in Lexington, Kentucky after visiting her ailing father in Columbia. I was only three. I seemed to recall Daddy announcing that Papa was dead, then running out of the room in tears. That ancient, primordial image from my childhood framed my hopes and fears.

Later in the summer, I wrote:

> My mom is dying
> and it is as hard to wrench
> words from this
> pen as it is to
> draw tears from my eyes.
> Only brief moments
> break through the
> armor and give access
> to the sadness.
>
> Telling my boss that I'd be going
> to Mom's bedside—
> this opens my heart.
>
> Reading my daughter's letter recalling
> a childhood visit with Granny—
> this opens my heart.
>
> Watching my wife bid perhaps
> a last farewell—
> this opens my heart.
>
> Listening to the hospice nurse
> describe final arrangements—
> this opens my heart.
>
> Now I face this
> uncertain certainty.
> She is blooming before
> our eyes and withering
> all at once.
> More present than ever
> and soon to be present
> only in our hearts.

11

Friday, September 21

I SLEEP, BUT NOT *particularly well. Once more, in the darkness of early morning, I find myself lucid dreaming. Again, the details escape me. I do remember riding this electrifying wave much longer and feeling myself navigating through a colorful abstract landscape. When I awaken, I am amazed to have experienced such powerful dreams on two consecutive nights.*

THERE'S SOMETHING ABOUT A *row of white wooden rocking chairs that simply says "Southern." In this case, I'm sitting not on a South Carolina veranda, but before a wide expanse of glass overlooking the green, forested landscape surrounding the Columbia International Airport. The waiting area in this postmodern colonial terminal is furnished with a curious mix of conventional airport seating and an abundance of Dixie rockers.*

I'm heading home. My stay in Columbia has been short. I have accomplished all that I had set out to do.

TIME

Time may not heal all wounds, but it does ease the pain. Time was both friend and enemy when I was processing Mom's death, both before and after its occurrence. We never knew how much time was left. That made each moment precious. That made the urgency of opening my heart with compassion all the more pressing. Reflecting on Mom then, as now, gave a perspective to the magnitude and finitude not only of her life but of the generations before and after—one more compelling reason to live a life of compassion. As the Beatles aptly sang, "Life is very short and there's no time for fussing and fighting, my friend." I take great solace from knowing that in many instances, my siblings and I were not consumed by regrets about the past or fears about the future. Instead, we managed to be present for Mom and each other. While at times we may have felt we were in a battle against the clock, Mom demonstrated how to live peacefully within one's limitations.

THAT FIRST SATURDAY IN August was Mom's "coming out party." It was the day that may have opened all of our hearts. Not knowing whether we were taking too literally the idea that Mom had forecast the time of her death, I cleared my calendar for the week—time well spent. She had much to say throughout that week.

ON SUNDAY, WHILE MOVING from topic to topic, Mom mentioned that she wished she had made more time for something. When I asked her to clarify, she replied,

> I think we should make more time for everything. . . . One day last week I had such fun. I was jumping around on the clock, changing the time. It didn't know what time it was, and I didn't. I told it, "It doesn't matter—next week I won't even be here."

She went on with her observations on the topic of time. They seemed deeply philosophical and quite perplexing. The gist of it was that she had changed her relationship with time, and with the clock. She was no longer watching the clock. Now, she was letting the clock watch her.

ON MONDAY, I ASKED Mom, "Is there anything you'd like me to write, that you'd like to share, that you haven't had a chance to say?"

She put her head down and touched her fingers to her forehead before replying. "Is there anything *you'd* like to share?"

She turned the question squarely back on me. I gave it some thought. What came to mind was one of my earliest memories of her. I was three years old. Mom was all dressed up to go to some function—probably a women's luncheon. She was wearing a hat with a veil—a netting of thin threads. I remember her bright red lipstick. She was the most beautiful part of my world. This was not an isolated event. We would make a game out of my kissing her goodbye through the veil. Of course, as I grew older, we

naturally grew apart, but in this moment, I wanted to tell her about one of
our closest moments. I said, "I remember when I was a little boy. I took your
beauty into my heart, and it's still there."

"That's really wonderful. Thank you."

I spoke to Mom of the typical challenges I had been dealing with in
my adolescence. I told her I was sorry for any pain I may have caused her.

"What a lovely thing to say to a mother. . . . How come we're going so
deep now?"

"Because we know we don't have a lot of time."

ON TUESDAY, MOM SPOKE loving words to Muff. "Do you know how much I
love you? . . . Does your mother know how much you love her? . . . Did you
give her enough time? I didn't give my mother enough time. You gave me
extra time today. . . . This is a fascinating theory—a whole essay of kisses."

ON WEDNESDAY, AN ERRAND to pick Jake up at LAX reinforced some of my
thoughts about the passage of time and the span of a life. I got to the International Arrivals terminal about twenty minutes before his flight landed
and at least an hour before he emerged from baggage claim and customs.
As I waited for Jake, I stood among a colorful throng awaiting flights from
many lands. It was a people-watcher's paradise. A procession of young and
old, large and small, able-bodied and feeble—all very much on display as
they searched for familiar faces.

I couldn't shake the images of Villa De Anza in counterpoint to this
spectacle. At the terminal, I saw a dark, shriveled woman sunken in a wheelchair—not appreciably different than some of Mom's cohabitants. There was
a white-haired Korean granny, joyous and tearful as little grandchildren
skipped gaily beside her. There was a tall, stately, independent, silver-haired
woman very purposefully going about her business. I was struck by the different capacities of the elderly travelers to transport themselves across the
room and across the world.

Curiously, I was even more keenly drawn to observing the young. I
noticed two teenage girls erupting gleefully at the arrival of their friend. The
three girls were cut very much from the same cloth—similar faces, similar
short, dark hair, similar GAP-ish clothes. The arriving party made such a
fuss, hugging and kissing the other two over the stainless-steel rail separating them, loudly exclaiming her surprise and delight at their presence. Their
dewy youth, their vibrancy, their unadulterated freshness—I kept flashing
back to the time in my mother's life when she was just as vigorous, and I
simultaneously flashed forward to the ultimate decay in these girls' lives.

There I stood, somewhere past the middle of this continuum, struggling to make sense out of all the excitement, the urgency, the sheer motion of people through space and time.

ON THURSDAY, AS I sat with Mom, I looked up at two family portraits hanging on the wall. One was of my grandmother, her siblings, and her parents in shades of grey—all posing stiffly, in formal attire, before a dark studio backdrop. The other was a color photo of Mom, Muff, Jeff, and me casually seated amidst the dune vegetation on a Saint Simons Island beach, the sea at our backs. Despite the contrasting images, I imagined how our fate is no different than that of our ancestors. One day, another generation will stare at our images with as little comprehension of who we are as we have of the preceding generations.

The second hand on Mom's clock-of-all-fives moved ahead with a steady beat. Back in her prolific days on Saint Simons Island, she had made the clock and others like it so she and her cronies could make every hour happy hour. "It's five o'clock somewhere!" she would exclaim, as she pumped a shot of vodka out of a giant Smirnoff bottle.

I glanced at Mom and inquired, "What are you smiling about?"

"I smiled all day yesterday and the day before, and I have no idea what I smiled about."

With the clock still ticking, I flipped back a few pages in my journal and read to Mom her thoughts about time from Saturday. Although this did not occur to me until later, it's possible that this was the first time she understood how I was documenting these days. When I was through, she asked me for the clock. Her gesture led me to understand that she really wanted my journal. How fascinating—she connected the recording of events with an instrument of time, or perhaps she merely wanted to read what she had said about letting the clock watch her. She held the journal in front of her, picked up my pen, and started "writing" indecipherably. Perhaps an expert graphologist with a microscope could have made some sense of the jagged series of marks she inscribed in my book. My best guess was that she wrote the word "you" repeatedly, or perhaps the words "go up." Her scribbling was harder to comprehend than her speech.

"Tell me what you are writing," I asked.

"I don't know yet. . . . I can't ask it of myself. . . . You have to ask me what I have on the paper."

"What do you have on the paper?"

"It's all done."

"What's all done?"

Bluestein family. Back row, left to right: Sam, Ida (Granny), Rachel.
Front row: Etta, Mary, Mayme, Lewis, Heince, c.1902

Doug (Yesh), Muff, Jeff, Mom,
Saint Simons Island, Georgia, 1987

"Thanks, Mom. Thanks for all the messages."

"Uh-huh." She nodded her head. With that, she closed her eyes. I thought for a second that perhaps this was it. Perhaps that was her intent; yet a few seconds later, her head moved to the side, and her eyes reopened.

"The before Tuesday message—do you want to know what it was from?"

I was stunned by the reference. Was she asking about her words, "Maybe next Tuesday would be a good time?" Did she realize that we thought that statement might be a literal forecast of her death? Eagerly, I said, "Yes."

"It was before Friday."

Hmmm . . . I supposed that could be interpreted in a variety of ways. Maybe she meant that things had changed since the Friday when she uttered that sentence. Debbie and I had come down. Jacob had arrived. Adam was due for a visit as well. My first inclination, however, was to think that perhaps Mom might be changing her "prediction" from Tuesday to Friday. I reminded her, "Today is Thursday. Fridays are like the fives on your clock—they keep coming around."

"Is that what it's like?"

"You're still in charge, Mom."

"All I have to do is accept it."

I patted her on the knee. "It's all good, Mom."

"If it isn't, you don't have to take it. . . . I've got some good stuff in these. . . . It's so funny—what I read the other day."

"What did you read?"

"I'll tell you if I remember. . . . "

A while later, Jake and I had a brief aside. Mom asked what we were mumbling about.

"Hospice."

"What's that?"

"People who help other people die. Do you want to talk about it?"

She followed up by asking Jake a question about his socks, even though he wasn't wearing any. Then they talked about his sandals. My interpretation was that Mom had successfully changed the subject. Then she "saw" someone behind the plant—Josh or Adam.

I told her, "Adam's coming tomorrow."

"I can't keep up with him."

Then she said "hello" to a butterfly she alone saw.

We took Mom down to lunch. I cut her sandwich into four triangles to make it more manageable for her. She didn't know what to do with it. "What should I do, God?" Perhaps she got an answer, because finally she started munching on it.

Later, back in the room, we waited for Nina to come and help Mom prepare for her nap. "Hi, Douglas. We had fun!"

Nina arrived, and as she wheeled Mom into the bathroom, Jake overheard Mom say to her, "It's such a pleasure to have them."

Jake and I left, grabbed lunch for ourselves, and went back to Muff's to pack for our return home. Muff got off work a bit early. After a while, the three of us headed back to Mom's for one last visit before Jake and I would take off. In the car, it hit me that this might be the last time I would see Mom. Slowly, I began to crumble. Tears came. I told Muff that I wasn't sure I could do this.

Nonetheless, by the time we got there, I had gathered my composure. Any other way would have been unacceptable to Mom. She eschewed teary farewells of any sort. I suspect that over the years, she fell apart inside whenever we headed off for college or moved away, but she would never let it show. Such displays were for lesser parents who, in her estimation, failed to protect their children's feelings. When Mom would drop us off at the airport, it was strictly "Bye, see ya," roll up the window, and drive off. I said to Muff that perhaps all those years of Mom's stoic farewells were preparation for this.

We went into Mom's room. She was sitting up in the wheelchair. Jake and Muff took the two club chairs and faced her. I sat on the edge of the bed, to her right. I set my journal on the bed behind her. Mom started asking about the paper. I didn't understand her at first. "Do you get the paper? Let's see you do it?"

Then it hit me that she might be asking about my journal again. She nodded when I picked it up. Apparently, my earlier reading had made a big impression on her. She clearly wanted me to be documenting the proceedings. Maybe she sensed that this was a piece of her legacy in the making.

For the most part, we sat quietly. At some point, it seemed to be too much work for her as well as for us to continuously clarify Mom's occasional comments.

The time was getting close to when Jake and I needed to leave for the airport. Just he and I were in the room with Mom when I pulled out the *Vidui* one more time. I held it in front of Mom as I read, in case she wanted to follow along. When I finished reading, I asked, "Amen?"

"I guess. . . . I don't know what the truth is, and what the Devil is."

I got up and told Mom we would be leaving now. At first, she protested a bit, suggesting there would be too much traffic. She eased up. We kissed her. "I love you, Mom."

"I didn't always know it."

"Well, it's like the moon. You don't always see it, but it's there."

"Thank you for coming. It meant a lot to me. It was a nice surprise."

I stood close to her, face to face, gazing at her soft, pale skin, and her searching eyes.

"Tell Alan goodbye. Tell Muffie, 'I'm glad you got him.'"

Like many a mother-in-law/son-in-law relationship, Mom and Alan's was tested from time to time. I was sure this blessing would be well received. I assured Mom that I would deliver it, and then, as she would have me do, I calmly said, "Bye, see ya," and left the room.

ONE OF THE GREAT benefits of time is the perspective it brings that is missing in the midst of a situation. Now, nearly twenty years after her death, I wonder what Mom would have said if she had had greater command of her faculties. Using a meditative technique that I learned from Rabbi Howard Avruhm Addison, I've imagined what her words might have been. At eighty-four years old, sensing the end drawing near, calmly enjoying every last drop of life, every last hug and kiss, she might have said something like this:

> I'm just glad to be alive and breathing, and capable of speech. I'm just happy, as always, to have any kind of words—they're all so beautiful.

> I feel so blessed to have such clarity about the sweeping arc of my life. I see so many people running around without that perspective, and I'm sad that they are missing the opportunity to fully enjoy just a little bit more of the brief gift of their lives.

> I have no fear. Rather, I have hopes and prayers that each of my children, their spouses, and their children find joy and blessing in every moment. In a broader sense, I wish the same for the world.

Time has also given me the chance to look at my brother's responses to the events of 2001 with greater compassion. I wonder how things between us might have been different if he had had the capacity to articulate his feelings and I had had the forbearance to hear him. I imagine him saying:

> Mom is dead. I don't have words for how I'm feeling. On top of that, the terrorism is frightening, and rather than taking care of myself, I feel obligated to tend to the feelings of my distraught congregation.

> I'm anxious about my performance in the upcoming High Holy Days. I'm anxious about moving to a new pulpit in another state

immediately after that. There's so much in flux right now. I just
want to get through it all as expeditiously as possible.

I'm practically numb because I can't bear the thought of actually feeling what I'm feeling. It's such a combination of remorse,
anger, grief, and fear that I'm shutting it all off as much as I
can. I don't like all the demands that are being placed upon me
from many directions, including from you. So I'm asking you,
brother, to cut me some slack. Just give me a little *rachmones*.

Just imagining what he might have requested of me is powerful and
transformative. It's nearly two decades since Jeff and I argued about Mom's
funeral, but I still find it very useful to empathize with him and appreciate
his perspective. I've heard that forgiveness for *another* is really a gift for
oneself. I have to agree.

None of us knows how much time we have. That's why the Psalmist
says, "Teach us to number our days that we may develop a heart of wisdom."
Striving to make each day count moves us toward wisdom. In the case of my
brother, we did not realize how few days he had ahead of him. How much
more I appreciate the effort I had made to reconcile with him in his lifetime.
Even so, almost a decade after his death I still find myself working on our
relationship.

YONIT

At the end of that extraordinary first week of August, I *kvelled* (felt delight)
over the depth of my connection with Mom. It had been a beautiful week.
I saw a side of my mother I had never seen before. I wasn't entirely sure of
what this sharing meant to her, but for me it was invaluable.

In much lore, the potent sun is deemed masculine and the passive
moon is considered feminine. But in some cultures, it's the opposite, and
that's how I perceived my parents. My mother had the firepower of the sun,
whereas my father—cool, quiet, often out of view—was more like the moon.
As an adult, I consciously sought to have my tides pulled by his gravity, his
quiet, reverent presence. The explosive, fiery essence of my mom was so
much a part of who I was that I had to push her away for many years to hear
more of my father's voice.

That week gave me something new—insight into a sweetness my
mother had rarely revealed. The gift I received was knowing that I had the
opportunity to draw from two sources of spirituality. I no longer needed
to deny the Mother in order to access parts of myself that I thought could

be reached only through the Father. I felt doubly blessed. I could see more clearly the grace, majesty, and holiness—different as they may have been— of both of my parents.

Almost a year before this, I had had a conversation with Rabbi Ezray about possibly changing my Hebrew name. I had just been laid off—again— from a Silicon Valley corporation. Every career crisis had offered me an opportunity to explore new ways of looking at my life. I knew that there was so much that I had not developed in my spirituality. I was not sure what I thought a new name would provide, but biblically, it had marked a new path for Avram, Sarai, and Yaacov to become Avraham, Sarah, and Yisrael.

I had been consecrated as *Yeshaya Dan ben harav Shimon*—Isaiah Dan, son of the rabbi Simon. Changes that I had considered included altering the *Yeshaya* to *Yeshayahu*—a preferred name for Isaiah—or replacing Dan, which means "judge," with something less "judgmental." I looked at a book of names and nothing really hit me. Over the months, I thought about it from time to time, but still with no direction.

A modern trend in Jewish naming has been to call people "son of" or "daughter of" not just the father, as our male-centric tradition would have it, but of the mother as well. For whatever reason, I had never been drawn to doing that myself. For one thing, my mother didn't even have a Hebrew name when I was born. Only many years later, when she and Dad were on sabbatical in Israel, did David Palombo, the artist with whom she worked, bestow upon her the Hebrew name *Yonit*.

One morning of that uplifting week, as I was out for my daily walk 'n' talk, I realized that my name change had been there all along. Suddenly, it seemed very fitting for me to honor the reverence and the *Yiddishkeit* of my mother by adopting her name as part of my Jewish heritage. I was so taken by the spirituality that emerged from her in those final days that adding her name to my already lengthy Hebrew name, becoming *Yeshaya Dan ben harav Shimon v'Yonit*, was more than a tribute to my dying mother. It also gave me a sense of wholeness, an integration of the attributes of both of my parents—two extremely different personalities that I had long struggled to harness within myself.

Moreover, I have recently learned that *Yonit* means dove. Among some cultures, doves carry rich spiritual symbolism. Some associate doves with motherhood because they are among the rare bird species that feed their chicks a form of milk. They are also considered to be links between intangible knowing such as dreams, and physical practicality such as the home. And, of course, they are symbols of peace. All of these add to the significance of adopting this name and enhance my connection to my mother.

12

October-November

During the Sukkot harvest *festival, the first week of October, I send Jeff a potted palm tree for his new office in Huntsville. It's part of a continued effort to cement my reconciliation with him.*

As the weeks pass, I think and write less and less about Mom's passing. Work and other projects capture my time and attention. It's hard to assess whether the relative inattentiveness to the mourning process is a manifestation of how thoroughly I've dealt with her death, or of simple denial. I'm not in the best position to judge. However, in an effort to be thorough about processing my grief, I avail myself of the services of Kara, the local grief-counseling agency. Since Debbie has volunteered there for many years, it's a little awkward for her and the agency to contemplate my seeking support there while preserving the customary level of confidentiality. After some internal conversations, they work that out.

A month to the day after Mom died, I go in to meet with a paid staff member to evaluate my needs. Finally, I am in a place that provides the comfort, privacy, permission, encouragement, sympathy, and support to let the tears flow—and flow they do. I tell my story and grab one tissue after another. This is just an initial intake session, not even actual counseling per se. Nonetheless, it provides most of the relief I am seeking.

From mid-October through the end of November, I meet with my assigned counselor four times. By then, using all of the criteria at his disposal, he and I reach the same conclusion—that I am dealing with Mom's passing sufficiently well, and need no further meetings.

IN THE BEGINNING OF *November, my job takes me to New York City. It works out that Debbie and I are able to add a long weekend getaway to the trip. One required stop for us is the World Trade Center. We take a subway to the Rector Street station and emerge a few blocks south of "ground zero," as many people are calling the site. I look a few blocks north at the familiar smoldering ruins. It gives me a sense of awe to be in physical proximity to this global icon of horror and devastation that so profoundly altered our family's ritual observance. At the same time, I don't feel quite able to connect to the reality of it.*

We observe the cranes, the smoke, the boarded windows, the abandoned shops—the many residual effects of the attacks. We chat with others—one Brooklyn police officer in particular, who has been on site since day one. We walk a wide perimeter around the devastation, moving through Battery Park and along the edge of the Hudson River immediately to the west. Perhaps the most tangible evidence of the powerful forces that were at work is the succession of large flatbed trucks hauling off massive pieces of twisted steel, one piece at a time.

We turn a corner and stumble upon a long, high pile of personal tributes to those who have perished. Teddy bears, photos, flowers, flyers, cards, letters—a vast array of remembrances for people whom others loved and lost. Until now, the enormity of the event as a whole has hindered my ability to connect with individual personal losses. This parallels my experience on September 11, when Mom's death was overshadowed by the day's events. After circling the acrid remains of the once-tallest structures on earth, taking in these unique personal stories, one-by-one, now magnifies the scale of the tragedy. We read many stories. While I am over to one side weeping over a card from a still-hopeful child to his missing dad, Debbie and others are asked by police to make way for a group of family members who are being escorted inside the restricted area. Surrounded by manifestations of grief on all sides, I turn to the east. Facing the rubble, I close my eyes and silently recite Kaddish. *I have begun the practice of reciting* Kaddish *each Shabbat during this year following Mom's death. It is Saturday morning, so I allow my prayer to serve that purpose, as well as an acknowledgement of the losses at hand. With the final phrase of* Kaddish, *I pray for* shalom, *peace throughout the world.*

> Oseh shalom bimromav, hu ya'aseh shalom aleinu v'al kol Yisrael, v'imru Amen.
> *May the one who creates peace on high bring peace to us and to all Israel. And we say: Amen*

It is a poignant and unexpected blessing to bear witness to and drink in the reality of the World Trade Center site. The catastrophe became such a part of our family's mourning experience. It is fitting to shed healing tears—not knowing or really caring for whom they are specifically shed. When we take in as much as we can, we resume our walk around the site. Half the day is gone. We then do the only sensible thing we can do—the Jewish response to grief. We take a cab to the 2nd Avenue Deli and have a feast of corned beef and pastrami sandwiches.

THE FOLLOWING SHABBAT HAPPENS *to be my father's* yahrzeit, *the anniversary of his death, which affords me the opportunity to recite Kaddish for both of my parents. I get to synagogue a little early—unusual for me, especially as our congregation has gone to longer services. I know that those who are observing* yahrzeit *and who are there at the beginning of the service frequently are given the honor of coming to the Torah to recite the blessings. I am eager for this honor, and readily accept it when invited to do so this morning.*

When the cantor calls me forward, I ascend the bimah. *My friend Dan is the Torah reader. I am very pleased to have him there by me. At first, in my fervor, I forget to kiss the Torah with my* tallit *(prayer shawl), then quickly do so. I recite the prayer from memory as my father taught me to over forty years ago. Dan chants the scriptural passage. Then I recite the prayer that follows the Torah reading.*

Having completed the sacred task of blessing the Torah, it is my turn to receive a mishaberach—*a personal blessing from the rabbi. The rabbi begins; then, as is customary, he leans over to listen to me whisper my Hebrew name in order for him to insert it at the appropriate spot in the blessing. While I have participated in this rite on many other occasions, I have been anticipating this particular moment since that August morning when I decided to honor Mom by adding her Hebrew name,* Yonit, *to mine. When the rabbi pauses for my name, I proudly utter* Yeshaya Dan ben harav Shimon Yonit. V'Yonit! *It seems proper and fitting that on my father's* yahrzeit, *I am making my first public declaration of my new, inclusive Hebrew name. I feel a sense of* shalem, *wholeness—from the same root as* shalom, *peace.*

SHABBAT

Shabbat is said to be a taste of heaven on earth. Growing up, our Shabbat table exemplified that. White linen, polished silver, glowing candles, a cut-glass decanter of wine, challah, a special meal, dessert! Attending the Shabbat service Dad led every Friday night, we would listen as a woman in the congregation recited the candle blessing which ended with a supplication for Sabbath joy, holiness, and peace. When Mom was that woman, the prayer had an added feature—the unmistakable charm of her southern drawl. This ritual is celebrated universally, and yet for over two decades, Mom and I were on opposite coasts, unable to share these blessings directly. My weekly Shabbat call to her was an important and compassionate bridge of that distance. In the weeks after Mom's death, I felt the void of no longer making that call. In October, I wrote:

> Before she moved to this coast it was easy.
> I'd wake up early—too early to talk to anyone in California—
> there would be a quiet moment, and I'd call Mom.
> In Georgia, even the late sleepers were up.
> I'd press the buttons by rote . . . .
> "Hi, Ma."
>
> When she moved to this time zone, to be closer to my sister,
> I'd have to wait three hours before I could call.
> By then I'd be in shul.
> So after shul,
> after lunch,
> after my nap, there would be a quiet moment.
> Feeling fulfilled in every other way, I'd pick up the phone,
> but never learned those numbers by heart . . . .
> "Hi, Ma."
>
> Today it was different in every way.
> I woke up early, and couldn't call.
> Sat quietly in shul, saying little more than *Kaddish*,
> had lunch,
> my nap, then a quiet moment.
> Feeling fulfilled in almost every way, until two words came from nowhere—
> and had no place to go.
> There would be no phone call this *Shabbes*
> or next
> or ever.
> What do I do with these quiet moments?
> What do I do with these words?
> "Hi, Ma."

PART 3
Mishpacha

משפחה
Connection

A whole essay of kisses.
—JEAN BALLON

CONNECTION

There are several Hebrew words that connote connection. With some poetic license, I've chosen *mishpacha*, literally "family," since for us, that has been the most important form of connection. At different times and in different formations, our family found opportunities to come together. Muff and I were naturally aligned—geographically as well as emotionally. Jeff and I had a gap to bridge, and fortunately, we were able to accomplish that. At the end of this challenging year, the three of us getting together, along with our families, proved to be the crowning moment.

Mom forged connections in many ways.

As it does for many people, the natural world provided a spiritual connection for her. During her twenty-five years living on Saint Simons Island, Mom made it a regular practice to walk the beach, enriching both body and spirit.

Throughout her life, Mom cemented relationships through the works of her hands. Even in death, many of her creations continue to fuse bonds with her descendants. The two cookbooks she edited provide a lasting legacy of her culinary skills. Her artwork—especially her mosaic work at the holocaust center in Jerusalem—continues to live on as one of her lasting gifts.

One of the most tender moments of 2001 came on the morning when I helped Mom recite the *Vidui*, the deathbed confessional that concludes with the words from Torah declaring the oneness of God and therefore the connectedness of everything. That oneness can be experienced in all directions—through connections to spirit, to community, to family, to one's soul. I was astounded to hear Mom declare her connection to God!

13

Wednesday, December 26

WE'RE FLYING HIGH AGAIN *today. Heading for a celebration of Mom's life to be held at Temple Beth Tefilloh in Brunswick, Georgia—an opportunity for Mom's community of twenty-five years and our family to come together and share in honoring her memory. This is the farewell tribute that eluded us in September.*

We arrive in Saint Simons late at night. I touch base with Muff and her family. They had rendezvoused with Jake at the Jacksonville airport and brought him up earlier in the evening. We meet them all at Doris Schlaer's place. Doris and Mom were close friends for decades and lived in adjacent condominium units. Every place we come to, every path we trace that was a part of Mom's world—and briefly Dad's as well—has a surreal quality to it. Muff, Alan, Josh, and Adam are staying at Doris's. My group is checked in at the Hampton Inn.

> *Turning down a dark winding road,*
> *Live Oak arms draped with Old Man's Beard*
> *Illuminated by headlights alone.*
> *A familiar dream—*
> *first and last images of an island paradise,*
> *punctuated by death.*
> *First seen while mourning Dad*
> *Now upon memorializing Mom.*
> *Sainted island of bittersweet memories*
> *beauty interminably intermingled with sadness.*
> *Pleasure and pain inseparable.*
> *Landscape immutably altered.*

PRAYER

Judaism places a strong emphasis on communal prayer. There are certain prayers that by Jewish law can only be said in the presence of the full ten-person *minyan*. In the case of the mourner's *Kaddish,* having a connection to the community is more than a requirement—it's a source of comfort. Nonetheless, at home and in formal synagogue worship there is always time available for personal prayer. Sometimes, a private, one-on-one connection to spirit is necessary and sufficient.

Mom's mom, Ida Bluestein Hymson, "Mama" to Mom, "Granny Hymson" to us, was the picture of a southern lady. She rarely left the house without hat, pearls, and white gloves. I always marveled how different she was, not only from my father's mother but also from all of the stereotypical Jewish grandmothers of my friends. She was the only one who spoke with a southern drawl rather than a Yiddish accent. She was born in the United States and always exhibited more of a New World attitude than the others did. She was fun. She had a mischievous sense of humor. My fondest memories of her are when she would come up from her home in South Carolina to visit us in New York. She would stay for weeks, sometimes months, playing gin rummy with us night after night while regaling us with stories of her youth.

Around 1963, when Granny would have been in her late seventies, she began writing her memoirs. One of her stories from 1925 describes how Mom narrowly escaped an early death.

> Jean, who was about eight, contracted pneumonia. At first, I took care of her myself. When the doctor advised me to apply ice bags to her, I was surprised as I always applied heat when the children had severe colds.
>
> Of course, we called in a nurse as soon as necessary, and I was told to keep out of the room after that. I didn't realize how ill Jean was. Oxygen tanks were brought into the room without my knowledge, and when she became worse and the doctor wanted to take her to the hospital, Charlie wrapped her in a blanket, and he and the doctor took care of that. Charlie explained to me that it would be better for me to remain at home with the children and not to worry, which I did.
>
> At the hospital the surgeon actually said that Jean could not stand an operation, but Dr. Cohen, our family doctor, insisted. God was with us. Dr. Cohen called Mr. Frankel, our druggist and a close friend, to fill the prescription for digitalis to be given in drops—a very dangerous thing if not perfectly accurate. When

Mr. Frankel noticed that the dosage was entirely too strong for a child, he called Dr. Cohen and it was corrected, which I believe actually saved Jean's life.

Charlie told me that for the first time in his life, he prayed. Thank God, the operation was successful, and she still wears the hole in her back to prove it. Jean's lung collapsed and for a long time looked almost like she would remain a cripple. Exercise, et cetera, cured that.

Ida Bluestein (Granny) Hymson, 1959

Granny Hymson's memoir provides a glimpse into the spiritual environment in which Mom was raised. Throughout her writings, Granny often cites the grace of God, and from personal experience, I know that she regularly prayed on behalf of loved ones. I don't know the exact language she used, but she always had us in her prayers. On the other hand, it wasn't until Charlie/Papa was in his forties that he claimed to have uttered his first prayer—kind of a foxhole conversion for him.

I don't know to what degree Mom was influenced by her parents' divergent attitudes toward prayer. Sure, Mom went to temple every Friday night and dutifully recited the *Union Prayer Book* by heart. But was she praying? We didn't talk about it much—not about prayer, nor about God. It wasn't until these last months of her life that I had any notion that she even had a spiritual side. Not that it wasn't there. It just wasn't revealed.

While Granny Hymson prayed often, and Papa/Charlie seemed to have done so at least once, the rest of my family's relationship to God—and to prayer, for that matter—remains a mystery.

I never met my father's father, but I imagine that he and Granny Ballon, fresh off the boat from Odessa, had pretty Old World views of God and prayer. They maintained a very observant Jewish household. Was the *zaide* (grandfather) I never met like Tevya from *Fiddler on the Roof*, always talking to God, or did he just *davven* (pray) by rote from the prayer book? It's mere speculation, but never having heard Granny Ballon invoke God's support, I don't imagine her husband did, either. He was a humble tailor, busy raising a family and trying to make a living. That wouldn't rule out having a spiritual life, of course. But while they kept a kosher home, observed many laws and rituals, and probably went to *shul* from time to time, it's my conjecture that the Ballons of Providence may not have had a deep spiritual connection beyond their routine observances. Moreover, according to my father, it was his rabbi who inspired him to enter the rabbinate, not his father.

As for my parents, all I know of Dad was what he demonstrated on the pulpit—"Turn to page 71 and rise for the Adoration." It was all pretty dry, devoid of much emotional or spiritual connection. His invocations and benedictions at public events often had more passion—but these, while they were addressed to God, seemed more like social or political statements than like prayers. He was among a generation of intellectual liberal rabbis. If any of them had a spiritual side, it was carefully cloaked by impeccable rhetoric. As his student in confirmation class, I heard him argue logically for God's existence. I just didn't see exactly what that belief meant to him. We never discussed his personal prayer life. Unlike Mom's, his death came suddenly, and did not allow time for shared final reflections.

Our family didn't talk about God. We didn't talk about prayer. We went to synagogue and read what was in the book. Anything else that was going on in the hearts, minds, or souls of my parents and my siblings, I wouldn't know.

I COMPARE THIS TO my personal view of prayer, developed over the years. We were taught to say prayers as children. In fact, some of my earliest memories are of Dad at my bedside, accompanying me in reciting the bedrock prayer of Judaism, the same *Sh'ma* that I recited with Mom toward the end of her life, declaring the oneness of God. My understanding of that oneness is still evolving.

The opportunity to connect to the ineffable is available in virtually any endeavor. The popular concept of mindfulness can be brought to anything, whether it be walking in the woods or washing the dishes. For me, mindfulness, moment-to-moment non-judgmental awareness, often brings a sense of awe and gratitude that can make an experience sacred. In Judaism, when we encounter such moments, we have a tradition of offering a prayer. There are many specific prayers expressing gratitude for many tangible and intangible gifts and experiences—waking up in the morning, eating various foods, seeing a rainbow, even going to the bathroom. When our entire family gathered in Saint Simons and shared a rare Shabbat dinner together, we recited the *Shehekhianu* prayer—giving thanks for arriving at that special moment.

To whom or what are we giving thanks? I'm not sure that matters. Being in a state of gratitude seems sufficient. Jews have no obligation to believe in a God that we that we don't believe in. We can believe, pretty much, in whatever we *want* to believe in, short of idolatry.

The *Baal Shem Tov*, the eighteenth-century founder of Hasidism, posited that there is nothing devoid of God's presence. As I sit writing this on a hill at a retreat center in Marin County, I see a rock sitting twenty feet from me. The energy of the universe is pulsing as much in that rock as in any other place. I may see the rock as another manifestation of God, but I am not tempted to give thanks or render praises *to* it—*for* it, perhaps. It makes no sense to me to pray to an inanimate object. The rock will not intervene in my life, but neither do I believe will *Adonai*, or any other epithet we use to describe the divine mystery that defies description.

Praying *to* God makes as much sense as praying *to* that rock. Yet I am the beneficiary of a rich liturgy that is replete with God-language. How do I receive the blessings of that heritage and use them in relevant, meaningful ways? By accepting God as a metaphor for the ineffable wonder and majesty of creation, by using God-language as a medium for expressing my awe and gratitude for existence, by allowing outward utterances of prayer to feed inward awareness of values and personal affirmations—that's how.

For me, prayer goes in two directions. Along with the inward focus, I like to reach out and feel connected to the vast, awesome spirit of the universe that is in a perpetual state of creation. There is an all-encompassing energy. There is a field. Whether there's a God or not is more a matter of semantics.

Simply meditating is sufficient to experience the divine flow in palpable ways, and just feeling part of the vast cosmic soup is plenty of theology for me. Ultimately, there is power in my ability to be in appreciation, to have empathy, to exhibit kindness and other attributes, and to float comfortably in a sea of surrender, with the peaceful awareness that while my actions have consequences, ultimately I am not in charge. That takes a lot of practice, and I know I have far to go. Oh, and occasionally I like to address the ineffable in God-language that Tevya and Granny Hymson would have understood. It can't hurt.

ON THAT FIRST MONDAY in August, after I obtained a copy of the *Vidui* from the local synagogue, I arrived in Mom's room eager to help her get that sense of oneness and wholeness that is inherent in the prayer. When I entered her room, as was most often the case, she was dressed, hair done, wearing a fresh coat of lipstick, sitting up in her wheelchair. We chatted a bit. I didn't wait long before introducing her to the *Vidui*. She showed familiarity with the term as applied to the High Holiday confessional. I reminded her that it says in *Pirke Avot* that you are to repent one day before your death, and since none of us knows what day that will be, the rabbis say we should live each day in a state of repentance. (Later, I would discover that a bedtime *vidui* is, indeed, a daily practice among observant Jews.)

I read this translation of the *Vidui* to her:

> Lord my God and God of the Universe, Creator of all that lives: although I pray for healing and continued life, still I know that I am mortal. Give me courage to accept whatever befalls me. If only my hands were clean and my heart pure! But, alas, I have committed many wrongs and left so much undone! And yet I also know the good I did or tried to do. May that goodness impart an eternal meaning to my life.
>
> Protector of the helpless, watch over my loved ones in whose souls my own is knit. You are my Rock and my Redeemer, the divine Source of mercy and truth.
>
> *B'yadoh afkeed rukhee b'ayt eeshan v'ah-eera.*
> *V'imrukhee g'vee-ah-tee Adonai lee, v'lo eerah.*
> Into Your hands I commend my spirit, both when I sleep and when I wake. Body and soul are Yours, and in Your presence, Lord, I cast off fear and am at rest.
>
> *Adonai melekh, Adonai mahlakh, Adonai yimlokh, l'olam va-ed.*
> The Lord reigns, the Lord will reign forever and ever.
>
> *Barukh shem kavod malkhutoh l'olam va-ed.*
> Blessed is God's glorious kingdom for ever and ever.

Adonai hu haElohim.
The Eternal Lord is God.

Sh'ma Yisra-el Adonai Elohaynu Adonai echad.
Hear, O Israel: the Lord is our God, the Lord is One!

The last sentence, the *Sh'ma*, so core to Judaism, is ideally the last words pious Jews utter with their final breath. I asked Mom how she felt. She said she was fine. "God and I are at one. . . . Isn't that what we're trying for?"

I was amazed at this uncharacteristic statement. No doubt it was indicative of a greater underlying piety than I ever knew Mom to have. As her old friend Marcia Saperstein said:

> Sit next to her during a service and one senses a different Jean—
> if you will, a reverent Jean. She has a commitment to Judaism
> and Jewishness which transcends her background.

I really didn't see that until those final weeks.

I informed Mom that I would be sharing our thoughts of these days with Jeff and with others. She replied, "It's very important that you and I share it with God."

That evening, the one that potentially would be her last, as I eased Mom into sleep, I sang an old campfire song to her, the one I used to sing to my children as part of their bedtime ritual:

> Now the day is done,
> All is still.
> Gently comes the night,
> By God's will.
> Glistening stars appear,
> Listening creatures hear us,
> Standing hand in hand
> Friendship's golden band,
> Father be with us,
> Through the night.

I hugged her and sang *Sh'ma* as I also would sing to the kids. Mom kissed the top of my head. When I finished, she looked up and said, "Let's give it fifteen minutes. That always worked with my babies."

I tiptoed away and sat in meditation for the fifteen minutes. I sat contemplating it all for fifteen more. I decided that stoicism on my part really wouldn't contribute much to the process, so I left my sleeping mother to grab dinner at a nearby restaurant.

When I returned to the Villa, I had to wait outside for the night attend-ant to return to the front desk and open the door. While I waited, I called home and filled Debbie in on the day's events. I told her that I had helped Mom go to sleep—whether she was to awaken was in God's hands. I didn't know what to pray for.

The closeness Mom and I had experienced that evening—it was the sort of dialogue that shouldn't end just as it was beginning. But could we even hope to connect in this way again? Was I asking for too much? I thought of the wisdom of Deepak Chopra—to act with "focused intention with detachment from results." My intention was peace, love, healing—I would wait and see what form it would take.

IN THE LAST WEEK of August, Debbie and I flew down to Riverside. Mom's color was better than I expected. Her speech, on the other hand, was largely incomprehensible. The few words we could discern made it clear to us that she was ready—at some level—to die. She seemed ahead of her body in this regard. The spirit was willing, but her flesh was a bit too strong.

This visit was part of a planned excursion on our way to La Jolla for Jake's White Coat Ceremony at UCSD Medical School, a formal induction into his class, witnessed by friends and family. Earlier in the week, when Muff called to say that she had been told that Mom would not last the day, it seemed that I might need to change our plans. The assessment Muff had received turned out to be inaccurate. Nonetheless, I left my work earlier than planned, telling people that I might not be back until September 10, figuring the time to transport Mom to South Carolina plus a week of *shiva*. It was a lot of guesswork.

Mom said she felt she was already dead. She said she wanted to do some work. I didn't quite know what she meant by that. My eyes fell upon the photocopy of the *Vidui* lying on the bottom shelf of her nightstand. I picked it up and sat close to her. This might be the last time I would read it to her. She must have been listening more attentively this time. She bristled at the words . . . *although I pray for healing and continued life* . . . So, I stopped and offered her an alternative way of reading them—that healing might be merely spiritual, and not physical, and that life might be continued through others or in a life to come. We worked on the whole prayer to make it more reflective of her condition and her feelings.

Mom was so ready. Her breathing was irregular—eight or nine deep breaths followed by very shallow breathing. Debbie, a nurse, recognized the pattern. She was so attentive, trickling water into Mom's mouth. Debbie asked me what Mom's favorite song was, thinking a tune would comfort her. I couldn't think of any. I put the radio on to the classical station. Debbie prompted me to hold Mom's hand. I turned down the radio, and, perhaps hoping for too much, got close to Mom, held her hand, and softly sang *Oseh Shalom*. I chanted its Hebrew words, then just its melody as a *niggun*. It seemed appropriate—a song of peace that I know she loved to sing at temple long ago when I was regularly at her side. I asked Debbie to soften the light in the room by closing the blinds. I continued to chant, first words from Psalm 122—

> For all of my brothers and friends,
> For all of my sisters and friends,
> Please let me ask,
> Please let me pray,
> Peace to you . . .

Then some famous words of Reb Nachman of Breslov—

> All the world is a narrow bridge,
> and above all is not to fear at all.

The chants brought comfort. I stroked Mom's head. Her breathing pattern continued.

When it was time to leave to join Muff and Alan for dinner, I did so with some reluctance and only after I heard Mom say that it was okay. I didn't get back until close to ten o'clock. By then, the staff had changed Mom's attire to a nightgown. It seemed to make little difference to me how she was dressed, given that she had become too weak to leave bed.

I lit the candle and turned off the lights. Again, I sat with Mom and chanted. Any fantasy I had about facilitating her passage went unrealized. After about forty-five minutes, she said she wanted to sleep, and I took that literally. She said something about tomorrow night. She also commented on my not singing with much pep—no doubt sensing how tired I was, or maybe she was just a bit bothered by my drone. I sat with her a bit longer, then lay out a comforter on the floor to go to sleep myself. My family was perplexed by my sleeping at Mom's on these occasions. If I had lived in Riverside, I don't suppose I would have done so for the weeks—months—on end when we were anticipating Mom's death. Since my visits were sporadic, and since I learned that it was a *mitzvah* to be at a person's side when they die, I wanted to make the most out of the little remaining time I had with her.

14

Thursday, December 27

Jake rises early to *join Josh and Adam for golf. For the rest of us, the day unfolds a little more slowly. By the time Becca and Shira—still functioning on Pacific time—rouse themselves, the morning is gone. I rush Debbie and the girls over to Doris's to connect with the rest of the clan while I peel off to phone in to a one o'clock work call that I am obligated to attend. An hour and a half later, when I finally get off the call, everyone is gone. Hoping to meet up with them, I set off on foot in the direction of the little shopping district just before the pier.*

I try to reach the others on their cell phones, keeping an eye out for them as I make my way down Mallery Street, but with no luck. Walking alone, I reflect on the times I went down this street on errands for Mom. There were always projects for me to do whenever I visited her—install a fan, hang a plant, build some shelves. I walk into Strother's hardware store, not to purchase, just to breathe in its familiar fragrances of sawn wood and machine oil and to listen to the languid drawl of the men at work there. If there were some simple hardware item that would somehow be symbolic of Mom, I would buy it, but nothing presents itself to me. I take "final strolls" in some of the tourist shops, but nothing tempts me there, either. Ultimately, I realize that no thing will capture for me the essence of the Saint Simons era.

It is a wintry day, certainly by Saint Simons standards. I walk out on the beloved pier—always a favorite destination. When I get to the end, I sit on the concrete ledge to take in the sea and to write. Even with my wool cap on, I need to pull the hood of my down jacket over my head for more protection from the chill wind. Earlier, I was a little resentful of having to be on the conference call, giving up precious hours of our brief family va-cation—especially today being our thirty-first wedding anniversary. Now, however, I am enjoying the solitude, the opportunity to reflect on being here and to create my own keepsake of the place.

I leave the pier and carefully step down over wet, oyster-shell-en-crusted rocks to get to the beach below. The tide is coming in. There is little beach to traverse. I walk its length, constantly aware of how much a part of Mom's world it once was. When I can walk no further, I clamber back up the rocks to the grassy ledge that sits above the beach. The stark white Saint Simons Island lighthouse—symbol of this shoreline community—looms above. I take a seat in one of the weathered wooden gazebos and continue my contemplation of what once was. Eventually, my cell phone signals to me that I have received a message. That's when I learn that the gang has been down on Mallery Street and the pier all afternoon—having lunch and taking in the shops. We must have just missed each other. They are all back at Doris's now, awaiting my return.

After I make my way back, we hang out for a while—the usual banter, the holiday bowl games—until my nuclear family parts company with the others to observe our tradition of dining out for our anniversary. Separating ourselves is a little odd, but I figure that over the course of the weekend, we'll have more than ample time together as the larger group. I want to enjoy this one special evening with just us. Besides, the Steinhar-ters want to go to a place popular for its large piles of shellfish—which I do not eat, and which is not even the best food on the island. There was a period of my life, after leaving for college, that I abandoned the kashrut *protocol of my childhood home; back then I would have heartily partaken in consumption of* treif. *Nearly twenty years later, however, after partici-pating in some adult Jewish studies and developing an enhanced level of religious identity, I returned to the discipline taught by my father. Muff and I kid. I say to her, "You guys will go out and have a good time." She responds, "Yeah, and you guys will go out and have a good meal!" And we do.*

> *strolling into J. C. Strother—*
> *lumber and hardware like any other,*
> *yet this was where she'd get some glue.*

> *turning into Frederick Station—*
> *beach pails and T-shirts like any other,*
> *yet this was where she'd buy a kite.*

ambling down the fishing pier—
weathered wood and seagull poop like any other,
yet this was where her crab traps hung.

stepping on shell-encrusted stones,
walking on her once beloved beach,
sneaker tracks on hard sand,
soon to vanish.
lighthouse, an aged beacon,
one day to shine no more.

this is all there is—sea, sand,
human marks on land.
moments linger,
captured for a while,
moments all we have,
all we may treasure,
until our grasp released,
no longer clings to mortal illusions,
reaches for shadows,
embracing all that's left behind,
all that lies beyond.

THE FRUIT OF HER HANDS

Mom had great artistic skill and talent. I cannot recall her ever making art for art's sake, but she brought her artful eye to creating beauty wherever she could. One might say that her artistic creations were a means of connecting her with others, much like the offerings of her kitchen. Virtually every object that she adorned was a gift of some kind for an individual or an institution.

Growing up in her household, we were witness to a succession of artistic endeavors in which she did not just dabble, but excelled. One might be tempted to call her a dilettante were it not for the fact that when she dove into a new venture, it was from the high board at the deep end and she scored darn close to a ten every time. No sooner had she mastered one medium than she was off to another.

I can recall as far back as the mid-1950s, when I was around seven years old, when her passion was painting on textiles—a poodle skirt for Muff, a Davey Crockett kerchief for me. Painting on white dinner plates was next. She made one for me that had a full color replication of the comic strip character Dennis the Menace—she often insinuated that I resembled the little tyke.

She expanded her mastery of ceramics by investing in a kiln, buying greenware dishes and sculptures, bisque-firing them, adorning them with glazes, and firing them into finished pieces. When Dad became a Boy Scout camp chaplain and the family got deeply into scouting, she would purchase little clay figurines of almost any imaginable object or animal, carve a hole in them, glaze them, fire them, and hand them over to us for a unique neckerchief slide collection.

There was hardly a craft in which she did not attain proficiency—sewing, knitting, crochet, rug hooking, calligraphy, decoupage, puffy paint—you name it. And she always had an inventive perspective. As youngsters, Muff and I watched a weekly interactive kid show called *Winky Dink and You.* The premise was that this cartoon character would need help from the viewer at home. In order to help, you had to order their special kit with a plastic sheet that stuck to your TV screen and some "special crayons" to draw on it. If, for example, Winky needed to cross a river, the viewer was given instructions on where to draw the lines that would become his bridge. We didn't have the kit, but that didn't stop Mom. She whipped out her tempera paints and brushes, and in our household, we painted directly on the TV screen!

To watch her throw herself into a craft project was inspiring. Often, this was on behalf of the temple or the sisterhood. If there was a convention or a gala event, she could churn out hundreds of centerpieces, programs, or other decorative items. She would set herself up at the dining room table and spit these things out like a one-woman assembly line. She loved the repetitive—almost meditative—nature of it. She would be putting glitter on place cards or twisting fabric into flower petals for hours on end.

In 1966, Mom and Dad went to Jerusalem for a six-month Sabbatical. Dad studied at the Hebrew Union College campus—and Mom linked up with David Palombo, one of Israel's most prominent artists, for an internship (although I doubt they called it that at the time). Much of the time, she cut stone into tiny pieces for Palombo's many mosaic projects, large and small. Clearly, she won Palombo's trust, because she had the honor not just of cutting tesserae, but of setting them into a prominent work of art at the entry to the Yad Vashem Holocaust Remembrance Center—a boulder upon which the inscription reads in Hebrew, French, and English—"Garden of the Righteous." It has been our family tradition on visits to Israel to pose for a photo by this marker.

Using her new-found mosaics skills, Mom replicated the signs of the Zodiac found at the ruins of the sixth century synagogue in Beit She'an, Israel. The twelve plaques were installed at our temple in West Hempstead. This was the magnum opus of her tenure with Palombo.

Muff at the Yad Vashem Holocaust Remembrance Center, Jerusalem, Israel, 1994

Mom displaying two of her reproductions of the Zodiac signs of Beit She'an, 1966

I owe my passion for art to Mom. I selected art electives throughout high school, majored in art in college, taught art for a year before enrolling in architecture school. Clearly, art was a gift I received from Mom that bound us together even when our tastes grew apart.

THE REBBETZIN'S SON

"Rabbi's Son" is a title I've always carried with me with a certain amount of weight. Many years after my father's death, with the aid of a Jungian therapist, I revealed to myself what had been painfully obvious to many others all along: I *hated* being the rabbi's son. It took a few more decades and my editing a book of Dad's sermons before I discovered I also *loved* being the rabbi's son. These revelations were equally true—the divine tension of opposites.

Meanwhile, there was an equally important but tacit title that I never really stopped to consider until now. I was not only the rabbi's son—I was Jean Ballon's son—the *rebbetzin's* son! That specific epithet was never used by me or others, but it was a mantle nonetheless—a covering, a protection at times, and a burden at others—being the son of my particular mother, Jean Ballon. Considering my contradictory feelings about being the rabbi's son, it follows that there would be equivalent mixed feelings about being the *rebbetzin's* son.

Relationships evolve. When I was a little boy, as they are to most children, my parents were gods. Mom treated me lovingly, and I returned her love. I had little awareness of the significance of Dad's position, nor of Mom's. As I grew older, I basked in the glow of their auras. Later, especially in my teens, some of that cachet wore thin. I keenly felt the downside of being in the spotlight, and of the frequent reminders that I failed to measure up to the expectations of the community, my parents, and, no doubt, myself.

At the same time, being the rabbi's and the *rebbetzin's* son provided me some swagger. Many people feel their synagogue is an extension of home. For me, I may have taken that too literally. I walked into the synagogue, and it wasn't like I *thought* I owned the place—I *did* own the place. Just ask me! It was mine. My dad built it. I think Mom had that same sense of ownership—either that or she just operated above the law in some ways. She must have felt some sense of agency—an extra right to be a little naughty. Not too many other congregants ever got the church giggles as she did. I followed suit.

In our family structure, Dad was cast as the heavy—serious, studious, hardworking, reverent, and, on top of that, pretty much out of the house day and night with congregational duties. At home, it was all about Mom. To be my mother's son was to be showered not just with affection but with excitement, zest, an appetite for many things, all—well, almost all—fun. She was nurturer and entertainer, purveyor of food, art, music, words, games, and crossword puzzles. That worked for me! We shared many interests. At the time, I tended to share more of her sensibilities than my Dad's—including a similar tendency to act out. We can't know how much of this was due to nature versus nurture, but we do know that I spent a much larger percentage of my youth under her direct influence than his.

My friends typically respected Dad. Some feared him, although I only recently became aware of that. When it came to Mom, my friends often raved about how much fun she was. I didn't quite know how to react to that, because at some level, I was in agreement. I was proud that Mom, with her position in the community, spread her joy of life to so many young people who continue to think fondly of her. At the same time, I suffered the embarrassment almost any kid would of knowing that my peers were aware of my mother in any way, favorably, or unfavorably—the typical adolescent push/pull.

Being the *rebbetzin's* son—at least in my case—meant spending a long time processing being the rabbi's son. Typically, a boy's transition to manhood demands some push away from the feminine and a concerted movement toward the masculine. I suspect that most young men go through a somewhat normal if painful process in this regard, and then come out the other side to have good relationships with both of their parents. My process was impeded somewhat by Dad's position and his relative inaccessibility, and then by his early death. I didn't become conscious that I needed and wanted a greater connection to my father until my early forties, when I attended *A Gathering for Men,* an all-day conference hosted by the poet Robert Bly, designed to help men access the full breadth of true masculinity. This was more than sixteen years after Dad was gone, about the same time that I discovered that I hated being the rabbi's son. Upon further consideration, I realize that that was about the *role,* not about the *man.* Any prior movement I had taken in Dad's direction was done without much clear intention, and as a result, likely was accompanied by some unconscious, inept, and abrasive pushing away from Mom.

My default position for many decades was to castigate both of my parents—Dad for being stern and unavailable, Mom for being permissive and too much of a presence; Dad for being too religious in a very public way, and Mom for being such an iconoclast—also in a very public way; and both of them for not figuring me out. It took a concerted effort on my part—one worth taking—to turn all of this around by examining my responsibility in every aspect of my perplexing "wonder years," having some *rachmones,* and exercising forgiveness for my parents being human. Now, as a father and grandfather, I recognize that parents bear some responsibility for how their children develop as human beings, but parents can only do so much. We all have free will—even children. Ultimately, children will make decisions that either support or undermine the best interests of themselves and others. Despite my occasional self-destructive behavior, my parents continued

to demonstrate patience, discretion, and love, even when I responded with
little of the same qualities.

WITH ALL THIS PUSHING and pulling, the seeds for reconnecting with both
of my parents were clearly sown in the summer of 2001. On one mid-
August morning, Jake and I paid Mom a visit. Entering Villa De Anza, I
saw familiar old faces—residents sitting up on couches and chairs lining the
lobby. I smiled and said hello as we walked briskly by to Room 139. Mom's
door was open as usual. Inside, she lay in bed, slightly paler and more drawn
than I remembered from the previous week, head back, snoring, in a deep
sleep. Jake and I sat for a while, saying little. He read. I wondered if I should
wake her. Finally, I stepped out of the room and called Debbie to get her
opinion. We agreed that in Mom's current state, she was likely to be sleeping
a lot—just about any time she was not actively engaged. I would wake her.
"Mom, we came to visit."

She startled a bit and opened her eyes very wide. Then she closed them,
and kept them closed with a tightness to her face that made me wonder if
she was silently weeping. She reopened her eyes. "I'm glad your contacts are
repaired."

I picked up the typed manuscript from the previous week's visit, and
told her that I had a nice account of our conversations.

"Good. I'll look at it when it's more real. I'm glad you are all contacting."

Mom had deteriorated in just a week. Most of her few utterances were
barely audible and far less understandable. Maybe it was because she had
just been awakened. In any case, she seemed weaker. I felt reluctant to com-
pel her to clarify what she was saying. It was asking too much. On the other
hand, I was not sure what response was more appropriate—to let her rest or
to help her communicate. So I asked, "Should we stay or let you rest?"

"If I knew the Hebrew language, I'd be much better."

With that response, I asked Jacob to hand me the photocopy of the
Vidui that I had left in the room last time. I read it. I kissed her forehead.

"Thank you. That was a good kiss. That was a better kiss than a lot of
them. . . . I wish a lot of Hebrews would accept this. . . . I was so proud when
I spoke Hebrew. . . ."

She started to drift back to sleep. I kissed her again and told her that
this would be a brief visit, that we had said much last week, that we would
let her rest, that Debbie and I planned to come down again in ten days, and
that Jeff might be out in two weeks.

"You're sweet to come. I like the way you treat your daddy."

I liked the sound of that, even if the meaning was somewhat cryptic. I knew she was talking to me, not Jake. Did she mean she liked the way I was treating my mommy? Did she see my actions as something I was doing as much for Dad as for her? Lovely imponderables.

I sat and took in the stillness for a few minutes. Then I gathered my things and signaled to Jake that it was time to leave. Walking out, I felt lighter than I had on some of the other occasions. Perhaps the work we did the previous week had created a sense of completion. Perhaps, even with the knowledge that I may have heard her words for the last time, I felt whole enough about our relationship that I could leave with little regret. Perhaps her invoking Daddy's name was a final blessing. Last time, she had given me a message for Alan and Muff. That was nice. I was glad to be worthy of the task. This week, she was tying our brief conversation back to my father, connecting me to both of my parents, much as I sought to do myself. If these were to be her final words to me, they were words that I would carry away with abiding satisfaction.

15

Friday, December 28

TODAY ISN'T STARTING AT *any faster pace than yesterday. At least I am unencumbered by any work responsibilities. By lunchtime, we are able to mobilize and get over to Doris's for a bowl of her homemade vegetable beef soup. After lunch, we all walk—where else, but back to the village and the pier. This time, the cell phone technology actually works and enables us to get together with Muff and her family who headed down there earlier.*

The weather is a lot more hospitable today. We find that we need little more than a couple of wooden benches along the small sea bluff to keep us occupied. We chat and fool around for hours. Adam and Josh walk to the pizzeria and bring back a large pie and some drinks. Josh and I end up partaking in a potentially deadly game on the beach—tossing the heavy aluminum pizza pan as our "Frisbee." The other main entertainment is a series of leg wrestling matches that have us in hysterics. I am able to conquer the young men, but ultimately fall victim to Alan's overpowering leg. He flips me so fast and so far, I nearly break my neck. So much for the fun and games.

As the sun begins its late afternoon descent, Jeff, Ann Lois, and Sara drive up. Jeff and Ann Lois are coming from Huntsville and picked Sara up at the Brunswick airport upon her arrival from Austin. When Jeff approaches, the assembled group all greet him with outstretched arms. His face wrinkles and tears well up in his eyes. Muff hugs him. Then I join in. It is the first moment of physical connection for the three of us since Mom's death—a reunion postponed by the national tragedy that

shunted part of our grief into a three-month period of suspended anima-
tion. Release is at hand.

We all linger in this sublime location for the waning minutes of the
afternoon. Jeff needs to take a stroll toward the lighthouse. I join him—re-
tracing one last time Mom's steps along the bluff. When we return to the
foot of the pier, the benches have cleared. We all gather again at Doris's.
Soon, Daniel arrives, having flown from Miami to Jacksonville and driven
the rest of the way up. The family circle is now complete, all of Mom's chil-
dren and grandchildren under one roof, for, as best as I can remember,
only the third time ever—Josh's bar mitzvah in 1986, Linda and Mike's
wedding in 1989, and now for this memorial in 2001.

Daniel, a chef by training, is immediately summoned to assist oth-
ers who have begun preparing Shabbat dinner. When all is ready, Muff
leads the lighting and blessing of the candles. Jeff taps me to lead the Kid-
dush over the wine. Then, he leads us all in blessing our children. Very
appropriately, Jeff also leads us in song and prayer with the Shehekhi-
anu—praising God for granting us life, sustaining us, and permitting us
to arrive at this moment in time. We make motzi (prayer for bread) over
the challah and enjoy a wonderful meal. (Doris will later comment that
she found nothing more beautiful that entire weekend than watching us
celebrate Shabbat together as we did that evening.)

After dinner, it is time for the older generation to turn in and the
younger generation to bond at the local hot spot. By all accounts, what
ensues for this gang of seven cousins is nothing short of unforgettable, but
what happens in Saint Simons stays in Saint Simons. As the kids are mak-
ing decisions about their evening, I call Linda in Columbia to coordinate
plans for Sunday. My cousin and I hardly believe that we have become
the alte kachers (somewhat impolite Yiddish for "old folks"). Where did
the years go?

BROTHERS

After 9/11, Jeff went rogue by initiating *shiva* without the rest of us. A few
days later, he added insult to injury by berating me for trying to schedule the
funeral at a reasonable time.

He and I made amends, but offenses incurred during such an emotional time are hard to erase, and the full repair of our relationship was a
continuing process. Several years later, while speaking with Rabbi Ezray of
my feelings about Jeff, I shared a poem entitled "Brothers" that I had written
decades before. Nat identified in my poem a clear expression of my yearning

to be better connected to Jeff. I myself had not fully recognized the extent of this yearning until the rabbi pointed it out.

He had a Schwinn Roadmaster
the kind with the fat tank
along the crossbar
that held batteries and
had a little round chrome button
to sound the horn

Some mornings
he let me sit sideways
along that crossbar
he seemed so big and strong
to pedal for the two of us
as we headed for the
Chestnut Street School—
a first-grader and
a big sixth-grader

That was the last time we were going
in the same direction at
the same time
the last time we were on
the same path

We've traced one another's
footsteps here and there
crossed paths on other occasions
often out of synch
going to or coming from
different places

There were places
of learning
of worship
of recreation
of work
of living—
a cat's cradle
of our travels
. . . our quests
through space and time

How glorious
to recall
a September morning
when we were going
the same way
as
brothers!

Jeff, five years my senior, followed Dad's footsteps as closely as pos-sible—Brown University, Hebrew Union College, military chaplaincy. But Jeff had a very different personality from Dad's—more akin to Mom's. He was a loud, wisecracking, mischievous rabbi's kid—as was I. His emotions occasionally got the best of him—as did mine. Recognizing how we were kindred spirits in many ways, I thought about how we might be able to grow closer.

In 2005, I asked Jeff what he thought about my joining him at Wild-acres, the site of his annual summer clergy offsite. He liked the idea. Soon after, I flew to Asheville, North Carolina, and the two of us drove the rest of the way through the Blue Ridge Mountains to the retreat center in the tiny community of Little Switzerland. The ride gave us time to be together, ahead of the days at the camp where we would be among Jeff's colleagues. In addition to heart-to-heart talks with Jeff, I also enjoyed connecting with his fellow clergy. It was a week rich with stimulating lectures and warm socialization.

In the summer of 2008, Jeff got a devastating diagnosis of incurable brain cancer. His cancer served to increase our sense of urgency for being there for each other. I took a measure of solace in the fact that I had already been making genuine steps to bond with Jeff. The foundation had been laid before his diagnosis; it wasn't a hasty reaction to his disease.

Despite the distance between Alabama and California, Jeff and I found ways to be with each other in the ensuing months. By October 2009, the cancer was progressively affecting his speech and mobility. Recalling our week at Wildacres, I invited him to come to a similar mountain refuge where I had often gone for study and camaraderie. The Isabella Freedman Jew-ish Retreat Center in rural Falls Village, Connecticut was hosting a Jewish men's retreat led by Rabbi Shawn Zevit. Jeff and I met in New York City and went up by train to be roommates at the retreat. It was phenomenal. Among the fifty men who had gathered together to create a sense of brotherhood, there we were—two *actual brothers* who came together and demonstrated care and love for one another.

For me, the most moving moment came on Shabbat morning after Shawn had spontaneously given me the honor of carrying the holy Torah around the assembly. In keeping with tradition, as I walked among the men, each took his *tzitzit*, the tasseled fringes of his prayer shawl, touched them to the Torah, and then, as a sign of honor and reverence, touched them to his mouth with a kiss. When I reached Jeff, *tzitzit* in hand, in addition to touching the Torah, he put the knotted threads to my forehead before tenderly kissing them.

As the months went on and his health worsened, we took every opportunity to see each other. In 2010, Jeff came out to California for Becca's wedding to Josh in June, and Jake's wedding to Alana in October. In August of 2010, between the two weddings, I overcame a desire for another strictly brother-to-brother visit and paid attention to a quiet voice inside that told me to ask Muff to join us at his home in Huntsville. Thankfully, she did—one of the few precious remaining times for the three of us to be together.

Jeff died of brain cancer on January 19, 2011. There was a huge memorial service attended by hundreds of people from all walks of the Huntsville community. I offered a eulogy recounting some of the wonderful times that we had had together, starting with memories of that glorious September morning.

16

Saturday, December 29

TODAY IS THE DAY, *with* the *events for which we have all gathered. Muff has arranged with photographer David Miller to meet us all at the Hampton Inn at 9:30 a.m. We have also received instructions from our new "matriarch" to wear khakis and solid shirts for a rare family portrait. We all assemble on time and appropriately attired. We follow David down Frederica Road to a beautiful grove of Live Oak trees bedecked with Old Man's Beard. David is a saint. He spends hours moving a sometimes-unruly bunch in different permutations—the whole clan, family units, siblings, cousins, spouses. Like Mom, we can be fun, and we can be outrageously ridiculous and naughty. He takes it all in stride, showing the utmost patience and professionalism in the face of buffoonery—such as the biggest clown, Adam, draping Old Man's Beard from his crotch or exposing his buttocks—that would have driven a lesser photographer to pack up his camera and go home. It is fun, and we leave eagerly awaiting the results.*

The main event—the memorial service for Mom—is scheduled for five o'clock at Temple Beth Tefilloh. At Jeff's request, we arrive at the temple early so he can assign parts to the "kids." Jeff has adapted a Havdalah service from Gates of Prayer *to suit our purposes. When I previewed it last night, I had some doubts about the prose. But in reality, with all the grandchildren reading their respective sections, it is right on target.*

Family portrait at Linda and Mike's wedding, Columbia, South Carolina, 1989.
Back, left to right: Alan, Jeff, Dan, Doug (Yesh), Debbie. Front: Josh, Muff, Adam,
Granny & Shira, Ann Lois, Becca, Sara, Jake.

Saint Simons Island, Georgia, 2001. Standing/back row, left to right: Jeff, Ann Lois,
Dan, Adam, Josh, Muff, Doug (Yesh), Jake, Debbie. Seated: Sara, Alan, Shira, Becca.

Jeff introduces the service by explaining the meaning of Havdalah— *separating the sacred day of rest and holiness from the mundane week- days. Jeff rightly feels this is an appropriate time for us to recognize the separation we are experiencing with Mom's death. Jeff tells us how Mom, throughout her life, consistently separated herself from the ordinary— even to the blessings she bestowed upon us before her death.*

He also uses the symbols of Havdalah—*wine, spices, and the braid- ed candle—to evoke awareness of Mom's attributes. In his words, "Wine gladdens the heart." With gladness, we can open our eyes to notice what is beautiful in life—just as Mom did. The aroma of the spices lingers after the Shabbat is gone, as does the memory of the departed soul—not only in our hearts, but also in the many artifacts Mom left behind. Moreover, the spice reminds us of her "distaste for the bland." The braided candle reminds us that "all qualities are paired"—that Mom had the power to warm our hearts* and *to scorch us with a word or a look.*

One by one, the grandchildren read passages or lead responsive readings from the service. I find myself unable to witness much of the service. The words Jeff chose and the delivery of the children open the gates of my tears. I sit there sobbing, feeling the deep healing warmth I missed at the funeral.

This memorial service allows Mom's former fellow congregants, col- leagues from the theater where she volunteered, and other friends and neighbors to come together to celebrate her life and to mourn her loss. This means a lot to everyone here—especially the family. We who were robbed of the opportunity to unite in our moment of grief have a second chance to do that, and we do it well under Jeff's leadership.

In addition to the collective experience of mourning and celebrat- ing Mom with her community, my siblings and I also have a personal stake in the event. After the strife in the days right after Mom's death, it is especially important for the three of us to physically get together, to be a family, and to embrace one another, not only to mend our relationships, but also to process our grief.

Following the Havdalah, *Rabbi Saul Rubin of Savannah speaks. For many years, Rabbi Rubin assumed the part-time pulpit that my father left vacant at Temple Beth Tefilloh following his death in 1974. Saul became a good friend of Mom over that time. He tells us how fitting he feels this service is because Mom had regularly and enthusiastically attended a* Havdalah Chavurah *(small fellowship group) at the temple. He says that despite the irreverent persona she often presented, Mom had a probing mind for Jewish studies. He calls upon the co-presidents of the Temple Sisterhood to make a special presentation. They posthumously recognize*

Mom with their annual "Woman of Valor" award. Then, a woman who had worked closely with Mom at The Island Players community theater speaks lovingly of her recollections. She presents some of the props that Mom had created at the theater as evidence of her handiwork. What I enjoy most throughout these presentations is that no one attempts to bestow sainthood upon Mom. Each person is willing to acknowledge Mom's idiosyncrasies as well as her strengths.

Then, it is my turn to speak. I read essentially the same pieces as at the funeral, so the thirty or so people outside the family who have gathered today can get a glimpse of that special time and the special quality of Mom's final days.

The moment is complete.

We adjourn to the social hall for refreshments and schmoozing. Among all the cakes, fruit, cheeses, and crackers, we set out some representative photos from Mom's life and, courtesy of Myra and Gene, a basket of See's Scotch Kisses.

I have a good talk with Rabbi Rubin. A few weeks ago, I sent him a transcript of my journals regarding Mom. He wrote back a lengthy message expressing a strong connection to what I described. He feels the story is a unique and sacred way to honor her, and he is especially pleased that Mom discovered and articulated such spiritual concepts in the closing phase of her life. As we chat, we find we have much in common.

I also enjoy chatting with Marie and Stan Rogat, old friends and fellow congregants from Dad's pulpit in New York. It is extremely gratifying to have the Rogats here, representing the deep roots of our family and religious life.

The memorial and the subsequent socializing are warm and enriching. I think we all listened to the words spoken about Mom with great pride. At the same time, it is a humbling experience to follow in the path of one who made such an indelible mark on the world around her.

Our mishpucha *(Yiddish equivalent of* mishpacha, *family), the out-of-town guests, and a few of Mom's closest friends go out for dinner at the Red Barn—a festive steak and seafood restaurant. The long table becomes stratified by age. The kids migrate to one end, Mom's generation to the other. I am sitting near the center. Ordinarily, I would order a Bloody Mary at a lively dinner such as this. For some reason, I opt to pass on alcohol this evening. It seems like I will fare better if I maintain full control of my mental and emotional faculties. Others are gleefully imbibing when seemingly from nowhere, shots of vodka show up at every place. I suspect the boys have something to do with it. I am correct. I ask what brand they ordered and am disappointed to learn it is Smirnoff. Then Josh explains that he wants to honor Granny with a round of her favorite drink—marvelously* chutzpadik *(audacious)—Granny would have totally approved.*

THE RABBI'S DAUGHTER

Describing the memorial service, I wrote in my journal the words: "The moment is complete." Little did I know how untrue that was. In the course of writing this book, I discovered that Muff had prepared remarks to share that day, and, for reasons known only to her, chose not to utter them. She didn't even inform us that she had penned them—just another example of her quiet presence sandwiched between her far more visible and audible brothers. Her words would truly have made the day complete. They are too eloquent to be left unshared.

> Mom never wanted a eulogy—so I will talk around her—by talking about us—her family and her community.
>
> On my refrigerator, I have a magnet affectionately given to me by my brother Doug, which says, and I paraphrase, "Oh shoot, I've turned into my mother." I won't question his intentions in giving it to me—nor can I argue the fact—though it's what you might call a mixed blessing. But I don't believe in gender discrimination, and just because they are males doesn't mean my brothers didn't fall as close to that tree as I did. Now we don't want to be negative, so we won't dwell on stubborn, sarcastic, extravagant, or the like. Rather, the things we learned to love.
>
> - We all love to cook and we value a good meal (maybe some more than others).
> - There's nothing more urgent on Sunday mornings than doing the *New York Times* crossword puzzle.
> - If you were to walk behind any one of us, you would notice our right foot kicking out to the side. (She didn't teach us that—just generously shared her genes.)
> - We are—none of us—afraid to say what's on our minds.
> - We know the importance of family, of education, of maintaining an active and involved life.
> - And above all, we treasure our Jewish heritage which—though it probably took Mom by surprise—was the mainstay of her life, whether in the densely Jewish environment of New York or this small but historic congregation in Brunswick.

Mom's beginnings in this community were rocky. Here less than three months when Dad died, twenty-seven years ago. But this congregation supported her and provided spiritual strength as well as an outlet for her energy. I imagine it was of mutual benefit, but we thank this congregation for the love, warmth, and faith you gave to Mom and to each of us over the years.

The other important part of her life in this community involved the theater, where she spent hundreds of hours and found a terrific venue for her creative spirit, a sense of community, and lasting friendships. Her love of art, beauty, and imagination is in all of us.

Not quite fifteen years ago, my brothers and I came for a weekend to celebrate Mom's 70th birthday. We commemorated it with a photo taken on the beach. This morning, with our spouses and children, we took another picture on this beautiful island in celebration of her entire life, well aware of what was missing—yet knowing her legacy is in our hands. We give meaning to her life by honoring her memory and upholding her faith.

If people say we have "become just like our mother," we take that as a compliment, and hope that we may continue to be worthy of being compared to her.

I sense that her natural humility prevented Muff from speaking at the tribute to our mother. She has always been the demure, unsung middle child. Therefore, I'd like to shine a light on my sister.

My relationship with Muff has evolved over the years. We were very close when we were young. As early as when I was three years old and Muff five, I remember the two of us lying on the living room carpet listening to the Magnavox console radio—our first TV was a few years away! Our favorite Saturday morning kids' program was *No School Today!* with Big John and Sparky. The theme song was "Teddy Bears' Picnic"—very spooky.

As school-age kids we had our private "chalkboard." We'd lie on our backs under the wooden living room coffee table, drawing on its underside, wincing as chalk dust fell into our eyes.

When Dad was a Boy Scout chaplain, the family stayed all summer in a quaint, knotty-pine-paneled cabin at the edge of the campgrounds (except for Jeff, who was of age to bunk in more rustic quarters with the scouts). Muff and I would look up at the various shaped knots in the walls and ceiling as one might look at clouds, talking about the abstract images we saw above and around us. Our favorite one looked like a Saint Bernard.

Back home, a Shabbat morning treat was slathering challah toast with sour cream. It was only after Becca came home from college that I discovered what she discovered: we seemed to be the only family who put sour cream on toast—a delicacy handed down by Mom. Muff and I had a childish contest of seeing who could eat their challah and sour cream slower, thereby being able to flaunt that last bite when the other had none. I still eat challah toast with sour cream, and think of Muff every time!

These and many other childhood memories set a foundation for a relationship that managed to withstand the horrors I perpetrated upon Muff during our adolescence. I suspect that it was raging hormones that led to my antagonism to the world in general and to my sister in particular. We became mortal enemies. I take full responsibility for the tension; I did everything I could think of to make her life miserable. We even got into physical fights. She felt it was fair to defend herself by clawing me with her ample fingernails. She was not wrong.

After those challenging high school years, we went off to college and managed to develop a mature friendship that has since never faltered. Unquestionably, we were drawn closer than ever through our collaboration in support of Mom in her final months.

17

Sunday, December 30

THIS MORNING, WE CARAVAN *up to Columbia. The drive is close to four hours. We head directly to the Hebrew Benevolent Society Cemetery where the local kin and a few friends meet us for a brief ceremony to unveil Mom's footstone. For many families, this ritual is performed eleven months after interment. Since among this group I alone had attended the funeral, and since another gathering of all of us at this remote location is unlikely, we take advantage of the circumstance to allow us all to share in a graveside ritual for Mom.*

I am returning to a familiar plot of ground. Still, it looks strangely different. The tent and chairs are gone. The mound of red clay and the green coverings—gone. For some reason, the shrubs that bordered one side of my mother's grave are gone as well—perhaps to make more room to inset the stone. I can't be sure.

After we all gather on this clear and chilly afternoon, Jeff asks me to pull aside the white, gauzy cloth that covers the marble slab. It comes up slowly, having been secured with more than the requisite number of nails embedded into the surrounding soil. The stone is carved with the same precise hand as Dad's adjacent stone. Other than the inscriptions, the only distinction between the two markers is the bright whiteness of the new one versus the gray patina of the older stone. Jeff had proposed a Hebrew/ English epitaph similar in theme to Dad's stone. Dad's reads: "The light of the righteous rejoiceth," from Proverbs. Mom's says: "Light is sown for the righteous," from Psalms—a phrase found in the Shabbat service which Mom would recite by heart.

In memory of Mom's spirit of irreverence, as well as her fondness for vodka, Josh and Adam succeed in getting Jeff's permission to "christen" the stone with a few last ounces of their Smirnoff. It definitely is in keeping with Mom's attitude of merging joyous with Jewish. We all have a laugh. We talk about the stones and the unusual BALLON marker spanning the head of the two graves. I relate my frustration with Mom's design decisions, noting, among other criticisms, the useless marble vase sitting on the base. I learn that the flowers that I had spontaneously stuffed into the empty vessel on the day of Mom's funeral were sent by Adam's boss. Today, it is Adam who rises to the occasion, providing one more bit of comic relief as he jams the now drained vodka bottle into the vacant vase.

The service is brief, straight out of Jeff's rabbi's manual. The assembled file back into their cars more quickly than they had arrived, heading straight to Linda's for lunch. I am in no particular hurry. I have come this distance twice in three months, but know not if or when I will return. I choose to linger alone at the foot of my parents' graves. Head bowed, all that fills my field of vision are the markers of the two people who gave me life—Rabbi Sidney Ballon and Jean Hymson Ballon. I remind myself, "They're not here, in this place." Yet I am drawn to the physical reminders of their absence. The magnitude of standing over their two markers has its own gravity, in every sense of the word. I feel tremendous weight—a tidal pull—and with the pull, the salty sea of my grief comes forth one more time—a sobbing I longed to feel. I open my eyes to watch my tears moisten the soil between the stones, but cannot see beyond the tears themselves. Debbie and Becca have stayed behind. I feel their comfort even as they give me space. The tears cease. I am done—for now—grateful for this return to my parents' final resting place—knowing that more grief still lies somewhere beyond my capacity to mourn.

Back at Linda's, we talk. We eat. We spend some rare moments together with our Carolina cousins. After lunch, everyone is either chatting in the kitchen or watching bowl games in the adjacent family room when I pull Muff and Jeff aside. I want a private word with them. I need to follow up on something Jeff, in his capacity as executor, mentioned on Saturday about making some charitable distributions from Mom's estate. It is a discussion that I do not want to engage in publicly, so we slip into the abandoned living room. In the moment, it doesn't occur to me that this brief interlude is the only time the three of us have been alone since Mother's Day. For that matter, there have been precious few such occurrences since our childhood.

We stand and talk in a close huddle. I am particularly concerned about what we will be giving to the memorial fund established by the

Island Players. Also playing in the back of my mind are some concerns I had not explicitly revealed about Jeff's approach to divvying up the funds. What I have not been able to do by phone and email over recent months is to be fully present with Jeff. His approach may be different from the one I would have chosen, but his sincerity is unquestioned. Any doubts I have quickly vanish—proof of the tremendous difference between real and virtual meetings. It takes us little time to reach agreement about the charitable disbursements. With that settled, I suddenly open my arms to my brother and sister and proclaim, "Group hug!" Instantly, there we are in a triangular embrace. The warmth of our wordless exchange envelopes us all immediately. Again, tears come, this time for all of us—a unique moment of sibling solidarity and support that outweighs all the discussions, negotiations, and occasional contention of the preceding months and perhaps years.

SOMEONE SUGGESTS THAT THE *five cousins present—Linda, Bubba, Jeff, Muff, and I—and our families gather on the front steps for a portrait. We all pile out there, and some friends snap away on several cameras. The ganza mishpucha (the whole family)—maybe not the biggest family, but still a lot of diverse personalities coming together in a place far from most of our homes, gathering with people who speak differently, and, I'm fairly sure, vote and pray differently—people we haven't seen in years. Still, we hug and kiss and share sacred moments. What force of nature drives us to assemble in this fashion? One has to wonder. In fact, one of the younger generation wondered this aloud earlier in the week, asking me, "Why am I here with these people?" It was a genuine inquiry and an absolutely great question.*

Our very full day—a caravan, a ritual observance, a family reunion—is now slipping away. Most of us are going to drive four or five more hours back down to Jacksonville for flights home tomorrow morning. It is time to hug and kiss once more, and hit the road. Quickly, we all disperse. In the confusion—some of us don't realize whom we will or will not see before we leave—not everyone says goodbye to everyone they would have wanted to. Such is life.

In an instant, Columbia is behind us. We head into the night and speed past Brunswick and Saint Simons Island a few hours later, watching them, too, fade quickly out of sight. The long weekend reunion is a microcosm of a family's life. One by one, we show up. We do some stuff together—laugh, cry, pray, eat. We have our moments—some loving, some angry, some meaningful, some frivolous. Then one by one, we are gone.

Left column, front to back: Shira, Becca, Jake, Debbie, Doug (Yesh), Ann Lois. Second column, front to back: Muff, Josh, Adam, Alan, Jeff. Third column, front to back: Kyle George, Hunter George, Linda Hymson George, Mike George, Dan. Right column, front to back: Ali Hymson, Staci Hymson, Paige Hymson, Kathy Hymson, Bubba Hymson, Sara. Columbia, South Carolina, 2001

KINSHIP

I have a natural tendency, a drive, toward kinship, an attraction to family connection. Kinship appears throughout our story, culminating in a sibling hug in my cousin's living room in Columbia, South Carolina. The underpinning of our connection was our common experience of being raised by one particular set of parents, in one particular Jewish home, steeped in the values of Jewish tradition and rituals for living in general, and for mourning in particular.

There is a broader sense of kinship among the extended family. My siblings and I have raised our families in different ways and in different environments. Nonetheless, we have a great sense of commonality. The next generation, our children, have a genuine connection to the stories, beliefs, and values of my family of origin. As the family tree extends, the differences become greater, and yet, mysteriously, a connection remains. The question "Why am I here with these people?" reflects the seeming randomness any one of us might feel about belonging to one clan or another. Membership seems arbitrary, especially when families are separated by great distances as well as contrasting cultural norms. This may be a microcosm of a grander idea. The rabbis suggest that Adam and Eve were created to remind us of the common origins of all humanity—so none of us can say we come from a greater lineage than another. We are all brethren.

18

Monday, December 31

A FUNNY THING HAPPENS *on the way home.*

At 8:30 this morning, I drive Jake from our motel to the Jacksonville airport a few miles away. His flight to San Diego leaves around ten o'clock. In the afternoon, Debbie, Becca, Shira, and I depart for Oakland. Our first stop is in Dallas, where we have to change planes. As we are walking the two or three gates to get to our connecting flight, I glance up at a man standing in front of a bank of flight information monitors. Even before I am conscious of whom I am looking at, I blurt out, "There's Jake." The circumstances that lead us to be in the same place at the same time are totally unanticipated. I don't think we could have planned a half-hour rendezvous in Dallas if we had tried. Nonetheless, it is great seeing and being with Jake again, even briefly.

So many people flow in and out of our lives. As a boy, I always marveled at parallel subway trains moving at slightly different speeds through the darkness under New York City. I would see a face and then watch it slowly move away out of sight. With some people, we connect—at home, at school, at work, at temple. We may see them again. We may not. In so many relationships, no matter how significant, the first and last meetings are unpredictable. However deep that connection may be, its imprint is eternal, its bond immeasurable, and without it, our lives would be incomplete.

LAST WORDS

The phone ringing in the morning darkness awakened us to certain bad news. The only question I heard Debbie utter was whether Mom had died yet. She had. I sat on the edge of the bed and recited the prayer that I learned for this moment:

> *Barukh atta Adonai, Elohaynu melekh ha-olam, dayan ha-emet.*
> Praised are You Adonai, Sovereign of the Universe, giver of truth.

I've never been entirely sure of the prayer's relevance. I was just grateful that Mom's struggle was over. That was praiseworthy. Then, I got up and ran around, somewhat confused. I wanted to know what the date was. I looked at the calendar in the kitchen—open to September. For some reason, I thought it was still August, so I ran to my office to look at the calendar there. Sure enough, it was September—Sunday, September 9, Elul 21 on the World Jewish Congress photo calendar that hung over my desk. The picture for the month was a marvelous building with special significance to our family—the Great Synagogue of Stockholm, the pulpit of my brother-in-law, Rabbi Morton Narrowe.

I called Muff. She was at Villa De Anza waiting for the mortuary to show up. We figured we'd be looking at a funeral Wednesday or Thursday in Columbia, depending on how quickly the mortuary moved. We didn't figure we could mobilize everyone any sooner than that.

I spent some time studying my calendar, determining what bases I needed to cover at work in order to attend the funeral, sit *shiva*, and observe Rosh Hashanah over the following ten days. I decided I would go to work Monday morning to lead a scheduled half-day meeting of our training committee. I also had a mid-day appointment in San Francisco with a "New Age" chiropractor to work on my ailing back, which had gone into severe spasm the preceding Thursday. My body had gone into shock way ahead of the rest of me.

After making decisions about my work week, I slept a bit more before meeting with my friend Dan to review our plans for leading an alternative Yom Kippur service at our synagogue later in the month. The rest of the day was a flurry of email and phone calls.

My final visit with Mom had been ten days earlier—one of those eerie nights sleeping on her floor. The hours unfolded with periodic ramblings and outbursts from Mom in her sleep. At dawn, she was talking from her dream state again. I sat by her. She let me know that she was awake and thirsty. I offered her water and juice that she readily drank. I decided to shower before the regular parade of attendants began showing up. When they arrived, I took the opportunity to go for a morning walk. I came back to the room. Mom had little to say.

At one point, I pulled out my shofar. We were in the middle of the Hebrew month of Elul when the horn is sounded each morning. I softly sounded it for Mom. Her eyes widened. She said nothing.

Later, Debbie joined us. She and I sat with Mom, much as we had on other visits, unaware that this would be the final one. When it was time for us to go, Mom seemed unenthusiastic about our imminent departure. But the last discernable words she spoke to us face to face were very clear. "Whatever you do, do it nicely."

Jean H. Ballon, c.2000

Afterword

"The unthinkable dream—you have to dream it yourself."

—JEAN BALLON

"Unthinkable dreams" was one of the bizarre concepts that my mother briefly addressed in her metaphysical, meandering, end-of-life conversations. In recent years, I have delved deeply into the nature and power of dreams, and I've come to realize that Mom was not off base in her choice of words. *Unthinkability* is fundamental to dreams, because dreams arise not from conscious thought, but from a much deeper place.

Thinking is the job of the *conscious* mind. Our thoughts are, by definition, a *conscious* activity—ask René Descartes. Our dreams, on the other hand, by their nature are *sub*conscious. Their purpose is to shine light on the hidden ideas, beliefs, and feelings that lie beneath consciousness. What powerful gifts the subconscious has for the conscious mind—*if* the conscious mind is willing and able to discover and learn from these "unthinkable" messages.

The idea that there is hidden meaning in the images of our subconscious, of our dreams, can actually be applied more broadly. There is little, if anything, that comes to our awareness that can't be mined for deeper meaning. What began as a book relating the story of my mother and her death is like any other collection of images that is subject to inquiry. It may, upon examination, become a source of greater truths. It was in that spirit that I not only wrote this story, but also read it, studied it, and dug deeply into it. I looked into the story of my mother as one might look into a dream: as a source of learning and something that held messages for me that had long escaped my attention. These messages were now available for my harvesting.

It feels appropriate that I would have allowed myself eighteen years (18 signifying "life" in Judaism) to evolve before embarking on this study of my mother's life and the events surrounding its end. I feel blessed that the years have given me some understanding of compassion, acceptance, and forgiveness that was not available to me back in 2001.

Everyone experiences alienation. Each of us has a unique way of thinking and being. Recognizing this provides a choice. We can take our differences and use them as a wedge—distancing ourselves from those we see as "other." Or we can see every person's uniqueness—as well as *their* sense of alienation—as the one thing we all share, allowing us not only to accept but to come together and honor our differences.

The alienation in each of us is often accompanied by a thirst, a search for a sense of connection to others and/or to something intangible. For some, a connection to others may be gained from a shared pursuit of the intangible, such as through art, music, nature, or religion. We may engage in any of these sublime interests and find that they bring us into community and relationship with others. Vice versa, our connection to others—spouse, family, friends, community—may lead to a sense of connection to the intangible—an ineffable spirit that lifts us collectively and individually. This thought is reflected in the words of the second-century sage Rabbi Akiva, who asserted that when two people in relationship are worthy, the Divine Presence—the *Shekhinah*—dwells between them.

The opposite of separation is connection. We seek connection in order to give and receive the comfort that is available in a relationship. Connection is what seekers seek. I'm a seeker. I have a natural thirst for pursuing what is hidden, what seems just out of reach. I seek connection among other seekers, and among non-seekers as well, and beyond that, at the cosmic level—connection to the ineffable. For me, this breeds a constant sense—an expectancy—that something profound is just around the corner, and the next corner, and the next. It's a bit like the enticing aroma of my mother's cooking drawing me ever closer to home. It leads me to prayer in its many forms: fixed prayer, spontaneous prayer, silence, meditation, chant, study—sitting, standing, walking—alone, with a partner, or in congregation. These all have the potential to enhance a sense of connection to others and to the Divine.

Empathy is a key component of connection. Empathy is much easier to manifest when one has had experiences similar to those of another person. It takes more effort to empathize with someone who is markedly different. I look at my parents—an example of the attraction of opposites if there ever was one—and surmise that their love must have been sustained by great compassion for one another's divergent styles

With empathy comes acceptance. With acceptance comes forgiveness. Nowhere was that more pronounced than in my relationship with my brother, when our disagreements were remedied through the acts of compassion and forgiveness that we bestowed upon one another.

When one is filled with harsh judgements, resentment, and anger, it's hard to see a path to compassion. Where to begin? It's a matter of consciousness that can be accessed in different ways. This is one more place where meditation is an important resource. Meditation is the practice of observing the mind dispassionately, without judgement, without striving or ego. It is like calisthenics for the soul. It prepares me for greater consciousness throughout the active parts of life. I used to cringe when colleagues spoke of *living from one's heart space*—until I was blessed to experience it myself! Cracking open my heart, even a little, has given me an opening to exercise greater compassion for myself and for others. It has given me the ability to express love in new ways.

The work I have done on my relationships with my parents, in writing both this and my earlier book—*A Precious Heritage*, an annotated collection of my father's sermons—is part of this continuous progression. Long after they were gone, I found new opportunities to hear them and appreciate their perspectives. I have also found a path to greater reconciliation with my brother. I've paused to imagine what he would say to me if he were still here. It's a gift not only to "hear" his voice but to be able to listen with greater empathy than I once could. It may seem odd that I have focused on my relationships with three close family members who no longer walk the earth. Yes, it's too late in one sense, but it's never too late in another. As author Mitch Albom has written in *Tuesdays With Morrie*, "Death ends a life, not a relationship." Forgiveness is healing for me, and I have to believe that it enhances my connections with the living as well.

Mom's parting words were "Whatever you do, do it nicely." I don't think she would have felt a great need to say that to Debbie. There aren't many nicer people around. I have to believe her instruction was directed more toward me. Mom knew me. I certainly heard her. I wrote the words down. For decades, I have been aware that this was the last thing she said directly to me. But I never took the words in deeply. They just seemed equivalent to an off-hand "Oh yeah, if you're going to make a sandwich, make a nice one." I didn't think of them as deep philosophy. I didn't hear them as "Whatever else you do, *be* nice!"

I have posited that to go from separation to connection, one must go through compassion. As I reflect on Mom's words now, wasn't that what she was saying? Whatever you do, if you don't exercise compassion, if you're not caring, if you're not *nice*, it doesn't count for very much.

Many people have stunning achievements for which they are greatly rewarded with money and fame. But if they're *not nice*, that attribute is part of their legacy too. I listen to my share of sports radio. I hear a lot of chatter about great athletes. Despite their achievements on the field or on the court, if they aren't nice people, the praise often falls short. People pay attention not only to how an athlete performs, but also to who the athlete is. This is demonstrated in other fields, as well. Just look at the entertainment industry, where the #MeToo movement has been calling to account otherwise successful men guilty of deplorable behavior.

If I am to take anything away from telling Mom's story, it would be a desire to exemplify her most life-affirming attributes while diminishing some less-endearing traits I may have inherited from her—not to mention the ones I have developed entirely of my own accord. I am painfully aware of how far short I fall in fulfilling Mom's wish for me to "do it nicely." No false modesty here. I have made incremental progress over the years, but I'm not done. I know Mom would agree. On one of those August mornings as I sat with her, the hospice social worker asked Mom if she had taught me a lot. Mom lucidly replied, "Yes, and he has a long way to go."

We are all capable of great and generous acts of the heart. We are all capable of the opposite. Dad often told the following parable that continues to resonate with me:

> The Hasidic rabbi of Sanz used to say: In my youth, when I was fired with the love of God, I thought I would convert the whole world to God. But soon I discovered that it would be quite enough to convert the people who live in my town. I tried for a long time but did not succeed. Then I realized that my program was still too ambitious, and I concentrated on the persons in my own household. But I could not convert them, either. Finally, it dawned on me: I must work on myself, so that I may give true service.

The only part of *tikkun olam*—repairing the world—that I have any control over, if I even have control over that, would be my own behavior. It's my intention to repair the world by repairing my heart. In an era where wanton disregard for authority, common decency, and the welfare of others is on display daily, simply being a good person seems insufficient. Feeling heartbreak watching the evening news from the comfort of my living room does little to overcome racial injustice, feed the hungry, or welcome the stranger, let alone repair a shattered and divided country. I must search more deeply in my heart for a call to action, lest I fall into hopelessness.

In 2014, I had an unforgettable experience at a weeklong workshop on Jewish spiritual chant with Shefa Gold, rabbi and self-described shaman. This was our fourth such session over eighteen months, so the participants had developed a close camaraderie. On the first evening of this final week, when we did our check-in, I surprised myself, and likely my classmates as well, by revealing how I felt I had been finding myself operating more from my heart space. I probably made air quotes as I said that, because even then, I found the term "heart space" to be a bit woo-woo. Little did I know that this week of spiritual practice would lead to a greater heart expansion than I could have imagined.

Each day of the workshop, participants and faculty provided a healing to a couple of our classmates chosen at random. One at a time, a student would lie on a mattress placed on the floor, while the rest of us huddled around her. (Surprise—I was the only guy in the workshop!) As we knelt beside the person, we were instructed to hold our palms open toward her to reflect the energy she was emitting, rather than sending our own energy. At the same time we chanted, "*Ma yakar chas'd'kha, Elohim*—How precious is your love, God."

All week I sat at the edge of the mattress and chanted as instructed. As each person finished receiving this healing, she would reflect on her experience, often with a tear or two rolling down the side of her cheek. The others would comment about the color emanations they saw or other metaphysical experiences. Shefa would comment on which angels, spirit guides, or otherworldly figures had shown up, what conversations she had had with them on a spiritual plane, and what healings had occurred.

All of this left me feeling somewhat alienated and bewildered. All I had done was chant. I saw no auras, felt no unusual vibes, and could not connect with anything I heard the others saying—that is until the final morning.

We gathered around the mattress for another healing circle. This time, my name was drawn. I was really delighted to have a turn at this. I had sort of hoped, perhaps even prayed, that I would be chosen. I lay there with a grin of anticipation on my face, eyes closed. The class held out their energy-reflecting palms toward me. The chanting in three-part harmony began—a choir of angels surrounding me. For several minutes, it seemed I was fairly well stuck in my head—trying to relax, meditate, and allow the flow of the divine spirit to enter—anything to get this profound religious experience that others had described. Nothing doing. My mind kept wandering and wondering: *Will I be the only one to just have a pretty song sung to me? What will I say when it's over—"Sorry, it didn't work!"*

Then, slowly, I detected a transformation in its incipient stages—a fleck of pink here, a dab of orange there. At first I envisioned these to be faint images of a crown, but I might have been wishfully imagining that. I took a deep breath. Eyes still closed, I sensed a feeling of surrender as shapes and colors started flowing with greater presence across my internal field of vision. Bright deep pink, orange, now surrounded by green, shapes moving, flowing, blue, yellow, but mostly that pink. A couple of times the canvas of colors seemed to be pushed slightly aside, revealing the black of outer space beyond, like an astronaut's view past Earth. I felt a surge of energy flowing through me.

This continued until, at Shefa's instruction, my classmates ceased chanting and placed their hands on me. I kept sensing the colors moving within me, as I thought, *Oh, no, no, no, no. Don't stop this. This is too much bliss.* Then Shefa had everyone raise their hands simultaneously, signaling the end.

I lay still, clinging to the mesmerizing images of light and beauty still dancing before my closed eyes. A few tears trickled down the side of my face. My lips briefly parted to whisper, "Thank you," as I lay there still stunned with rapture. Finally, with a sigh, I watched the colors fade. I opened my eyes, continuing to lie in mute awe.

Shefa asked if I wanted to know who visited me.

Still in a whisper, "Yes, of course."

"Your father and your brother," she stated. "They said—well they didn't speak it directly in words—but they said to direct energy to the heart space. Did they have heart problems?" Dad died during coronary by-pass surgery, and Jeff had had a quintuple by-pass. Shefa added that in addition to opening my heart on a spiritual level, they had acted to shift my DNA physically and energetically.

Remembering my check-in, Shefa looked down on me lying on the mattress and playfully teased, to the amusement of all, "Heart space, heart space, heart space." Shefa added that my father and brother approved of what I was doing.

Finally, I was able to speak. "There were a lot of colors."

Others concurred. One classmate said I was the first one she had seen emanate such dramatic colors—a yellow glow, then black lightning, accompanied by a sense of sadness. Another student described waves of energy coming off of me—powerful waves, like an ocean. She was drawn to come as close as she could without touching me, because she felt it would be electric. A third person found herself moving back, because the energy field was growing.

I gave my own account of the experience, describing the colors I had seen.

"That's crazy stuff," I added.

"That's normal to me!" Shefa responded.

I wondered what I would do with this experience, feeling that it would take some time to find out. An answer came as soon as the next morning's Shabbat service. When I prayed the *Amidah* silent prayer, the colors returned—although with less intensity than the day before. To this day there are times, mostly during meditation or prayer, when subdued glimpses of the colors return, reminding me that I am part of an amazing, unending, incomprehensible energy field.

At the time, I was fairly focused on the physical aspect of the blessing for my heart. Today, more than six years later, when, *keinehora* (the Jewish equivalent of "knock on wood"), stress tests have shown my cardiac muscle to be strong, I realize that that probably was not what Dad and Jeff were concerned about. It was more likely my capacity for compassion—my ability to pass a *rachmones* stress test—that bothered them. It seems I was there to receive blessings, not as much for the heart that powers my circulatory system, but for the heart that powers my soul.

How did this happen? I set out to tell the story of my mother's death and I end up with a tale about the spirits of my father and my brother, and the transformation of my heart? Maybe this is not so surprising, as I recognize how central in my life all three of these departed souls have been from the moment I was born until this day; how many lessons they have provided and continue to provide for me; and how much my heart yearns to keep them alive by sustaining our memories of them. Dad and Jeff were taken from us much too soon—both in their sixties when they died. Mom was blessed with eighty-four years of life. She may have been ready, but it was still too soon for us.

Mom did not want to be eulogized, perhaps because she was too keenly aware of her shortcomings. Or perhaps because she understood that the sum of anyone's life is far greater than words can capture. She was flawed, as we all are. She was also larger than life, constantly challenging herself and those around her to relish all of life's bounty. Mom's many talents—especially in the arts and in the kitchen—were the media through which she expressed her profound and undying love of her family, her friends, and of life itself. In the end, she wrapped it all up in an uncharacteristically serene appreciation of her family and her Jewish heritage.

May her memory be a lasting blessing.

Appendix

RECIPES

No book about Jean Ballon would be complete without including some of her recipes. In 1974, she and some other women from Nassau Community Temple in West Hempstead, Long Island, and Temple Emanuel in nearby Lynbrook, published a Sisterhood cookbook called *From Generation to Generation.* As Mom pointed out, the recipes were not necessarily original to their contributors; the book was just a compilation of favorites. Truth be told, some of the named "contributors" may not have even heard of the recipes for which they were given credit. That was because Mom wanted to include a great many of her own favorites, but she didn't want people to see her name on every page—so she occasionally inserted the names of random friends or relatives!

Mom clipped art from magazines and other publications in an era before "clipart" was a thing. She literally cut out and pasted most of the illustrations in the book, and drew a few of her own.

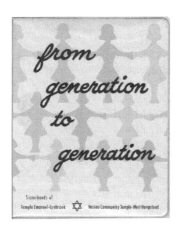

As a newlywed, Granny Hymson overcooked a dinner of calves' liver. Virtually every recipe for this dish warns against doing just that, but wanting to spare his bride's feelings, Papa/Charlie exclaimed, "That's just the way I like it!" For decades, Granny would set aside his portion of liver and cook it until it was barely edible. Finally, one time when Mom served Papa properly cooked liver, he couldn't contain his satisfaction—and the truth was finally revealed. I'm not naïve enough to believe that anyone I know is about to make this dish, but I feel compelled to tell this piece of family lore.

123

SAUTEED CALF'S LIVER   JEAN BALLON

```
         1 LB CALF'S LIVER, 1/4" SLICES
         SALT, PEPPER AND FLOUR
         BUTTER
         SAUTEED ONIONS, IF DESIRED
         SAUTEED MUSHROOMS, IF DESIRED

SEASON LIVER SLICES WITH SALT AND PEPPER.  DIP
IN FLOUR, THEN SHAKE OFF EXCESS.  MELT 2 TBS
BUTTER IN SKILLET; WHEN FOAM SUBSIDES ADD LIVER
AND COOK FOR 2 MIN ON EACH SIDE OR UNTIL SLICES
ARE LIGHT BROWN, TURNING THEM WITH KITCHEN
TONGS.  DO NOT OVERCOOK.  REMOVE LIVER TO HEATED
PLATTER AND SCATTER ONIONS, MUSHROOMS OVER AND
SERVE AT ONCE.

JUST BEFORE SERVING, POUR 1/2 C WHITE WINE
INTO SKILLET FOR A GOOD SAUCE.  SERVE WITH
RICE.  SLICED APPLES, SAUTEED AND KEPT WARM
ARE SO GOOD WITH LIVER.
```

LIVER
$2.09 lb

"I want it for dinner . . . not a transplant."

Her signature dish—not easily replicated—was Mom's southern fried chicken, a product of her loving perseverance as she stood diligently over her perfectly seasoned cast iron skillet, coaxing each piece into perfection. Visiting her in coastal Georgia, I would ask where one could find the best fried chicken around. It was disheartening to hear her reply, "Popeyes."

<u>FRIED CHICKEN, Y'ALL</u>   <u>JEAN BALLON</u>   167

    FRYERS, CUT UP
    BISQUICK
    SALT, PEPPER AND POULTRY
        SEASONING

CUT CHICKEN INTO SMALLER PIECES THAN USUAL.
(THE MORE CRUST THE BETTER.) DROP WET CHICKEN
INTO BAG OF BISQUICK WHICH HAS BEEN MIXED WITH
SEASONING...ONE PIECE AT A TIME...MAKING SURE
IT IS WELL COATED. FRY IN DEEP FAT WHICH IS
MODERATELY HOT. FRY COVERED ABOUT 5 MIN,
REMOVE COVER FOR AN ADDITIONAL 5 MIN. TURN AND
REPEAT. IT SHOULD TAKE ABOUT 25 MIN TO COM-
PLETELY BROWN LARGE PIECES. A LITTLE LESS FOR
SMALLER ONES. KEEP TURNING DURING THIS TIME..
IT BROWNS MORE EVENLY. DRAIN ON PLENTY OF
PAPER TOWELS.

<u>TIP:</u> A GOOD OLE SO'THEN COOK ONCE TOLD ME TO
TURN FRIED CHICKEN OFTEN. IT MAKES THE CRUST
BETTER. NEVER COVER OR PUT INTO OVEN AFTER IT
IS DONE. IT WILL GO LIMP. IF YOU MUST KEEP IT
HOT, LEAVE OVEN DOOR AJAR OR PUT IN OPEN ROTO-
BROIL ON LOW HEAT.

Now we come to one of her truly unique and superlative family-revered recipes—Mom's juicy, tangy turkey. There are other ways to make excellent turkey, but none better than this. Although she did not describe this trick in her instructions, as she carved the bird, Mom always placed the slices of turkey right back in the roasting pan where they soaked in the warm juices rather than drying out on a platter.

171

OLD FASHIONED TURKEY   JEAN BALLON

                    TURKEY, SEASONED INSIDE AND OUT
                    PLENTY OF ONIONS
                    PLENTY OF CELERY
                    PLENTY OF BUTTER OR OLEO
                    1/4 - 1/2 C FLOUR
                    1 C CHICKEN BROTH
                    1 C ORANGE JUICE
                    1/2 C DRY WHITE WINE

DICE AND SAUTEE VEGETABLES IN OLEO. ADD
FLOUR STIRRING UNTIL SMOOTH. REMOVE FROM FIRE.
GRADUALLY ADD LIQUIDS. NOW BATHE TURKEY WITH
THIS MIXTURE. ADDITIONAL BROTH MAY BE
ADDED DURING BAKING. BAKE AT 325°, COVERED
AT FIRST. IN LAST HOUR, UNCOVER AND BASTE
OFTEN. WINE AND ORANGE JUICE MAY BE ELIMIN-
ATED AND BROTH USED IN ITS STEAD, BUT WE LOVE
IT THIS WAY...SO JUICY AND PLENTY OF REAL GOOD
GRAVY. GREAT FOR CAPONS OR ROASTERS, TOO.

Mom was a one-woman blintz factory: pouring the batter and cooking one crepe while filling and rolling the previous one in a seamless solo assembly line. The "Etta" in the recipe's name was Aunt Etta, Granny Hymson's sister.

213

ETTA'S CHEESE BLINTZES   JEAN BALLON

BATTER: 3 EGGS, PLUS 1 WHITE
                   1/2 C WATER
                   1/2 C MILK
                   2-3 TBS MELTED BUTTER
                   1 C FLOUR
                   1/4 TSP BAKING POWDER
                   1/2 TSP SALT

FILLING: 8 OZ PKG FARMER CHEESE
                   8 OZ POT CHEESE
                   1 EGG YOLK
                   2-3 TBS MELTED BUTTER
                   1/2 TSP SALT
                   2 TBS SUGAR

BEAT EGGS; ADD LIQUID, THEN FLOUR AND RE-
MAINING INGREDIENTS. BATTER SHOULD BE THIN
AND OF POURING CONSISTENCY. OIL 6" IRON
OR OMELET PAN OVER MED-HIGH HEAT. USING
A PLASTIC COFFEE MEASURE, TILT PAN AS YOU POUR
ONE MEASUREFUL OF BATTER, MAKING SURE THE
ENTIRE BOTTOM OF PAN IS COVERED. COOK UNTIL
TOP OF PANCAKE APPEARS ALMOST DRY. DO NOT
TURN OVER. HAVE CHEESE FILLING PREPARED SO
YOU CAN FILL IMMEDIATELY AFTER YOU PUT THE
NEXT PANCAKE INTO PAN. IT SHOULD TAKE
YOU JUST THE AMOUNT OF TIME IT WILL TAKE
THE PANCAKE TO COOK. THIS AVOIDS STACKING
PANCAKES.

PANCAKES MAY BE FROZEN EITHER FILLED OR
NOT FILLED. IF FROZEN UNFILLED, SEPARATE
BY PUTTING TWO PIECES OF WAXED PAPER
BETWEEN EACH PANCAKE. IF FILLED, LAYER
WITH WAXED PAPER BETWEEN. FRY EITHER
THAWED OR UNTHAWED. BEST FRIED IN BUTTER
AND OIL MIXED.

This is my choice for "Best in Show." The key is the dough. Not too soft. Not too hard. Like a perfect cookie. The brown sugar creates a great flavor. It almost doesn't matter what filling you use with it—Nutella is a recent addition to the repertoire. Best gobbled up immediately. Like French bread, any that survive will lose their perfect texture if stored in a sealed container.

297

HAMANTASHEN   JEAN BALLON

COOKIE DOUGH

2/3 C BUTTER
1 C BROWN SUGAR, FIRMLY PACKED
1 EGG
1 TSP VANILLA
1/2 TSP LEMON EXTRACT
    (optional)
1/3 C MILK
3 C FLOUR
3 TSP BAKING POWDER

CREAM TOGETHER FIRST 5 INGREDIENTS. SIFT
TOGETHER FLOUR AND BAKING POWDER AND ADD
ALTERNATELY WITH MILK. CHILL DOUGH. ROLL
ON LIGHTLY FLOURED BOARD OR BETWEEN WAXED
PAPER. CUT CIRCLE 21/2". FILL WITH TSP
OF FILLING. PULL UP 3 SIDES AND PINCH
TOGETHER. BAKE IN 350° OVEN FOR 25-30
MIN.

FILLING

1 C PRUNES, PITTED or CHOPPED*
1 C RAISINS
1/2 C SUGAR
1/2 C WATER
1 TBS FLOUR
2 TBS LEMON JUICE
CHOPPED NUTS
1 TBS BUTTER

PUT FIRST 7 INGREDIENTS INTO SAUCE PAN AND COOK
GENTLY UNTIL THICKENED. STIR OCCASIONALLY TO
KEEP FROM STICKING. REMOVE FROM HEAT. ADD
BUTTER.

ALTERNATE SUGGESTION: OR TRY PREPARED PRUNE
FILLINGS AS PRUNE BUTTER. ADD NUTS, RAISINS,
GRATED ORANGE OR LEMON PEEL, ORANGE OR LEMON
MARMALADE, PLUM PRESERVES ETC.

*Dried apricots may be used in place
 of prunes or in addition to prunes.

You won't find a better honey cake than this. For starters, it's moist and flavorful, unlike 99% of the rest of them. It's a mystery that this recipe didn't make it into the cookbook. This is a well-worn page that we inserted later. Debbie thinks this is the best recipe of all.

```
HONEY CAKE                        JEAN BALLON

        1 3/4 c orange blossom honey
        1 c strong coffee
        2 tbs brandy (Coffee liqueur or
              B & B, etc)
        4 eggs
        1/4 scant c vegetable oil
        1 c brown sugar
        3 1/2-4 c flour
        3 tsp baking powder
        1 tsp baking soda
        2 tsp ginger
        1 tsp each, cinnamon,allspice,
              nutmeg
        1 c chopped walnuts or pecans
        1 c raisins
        2-3 pieces of crystallized ginger, d
              diced thin

Add coffee to honey and bring to boil.  Cool.
Add brandy.  Beat eggs and stir in oil, then su
sugar. Mix all dry ingredients, including
fruit and nuts.  Add to egg mixture alter-
nately with honey mixture.  Mix well and
ppur into greased loaf pan.  Bake at 300
for about 1 hr.  When done invert pan and
cool.

Makes 2 large loaf cakes..3 aluminum foil
(like Sara Lee) loaf pans...and 1 large
tube pan..

 I just mix everything. Stir and beat like
 hell with electric mixer for as long as I
have to in order to get it light and
fluffy.  Then add fruit and nuts gently
tossed with some of the flour.

I find it takes 1 hr and 14 min for two
large or 1 large cake.  About 1 hr for
3 smaller ones.
```

As long as you must cook, you might as well make it an adventure.

—JEAN BALLON

Made in the USA
Las Vegas, NV
08 October 2021